ORDER IN CHAOS

Why Work Feels Harder Than It Should and What's Really Driving It

ORDER IN CHAOS

Why Work Feels Harder Than It Should and What's Really Driving It

JOHN CZAPKO

Published independently by:

Credible Ink
Greensboro, NC
www.credible.ink

Paperback ISBN: 979-8-9935769-3-0
Hardcover ISBN: 979-8-9935769-4-7
eBook ISBN: 979-8-9935769-5-4

First Edition

Printed in the United States of America

To God, To Diana, To CJ and Hayley,
And, to my parents, who gave me the first structure that made
everything else possible.

Acknowledgments

This book took shape through many early mornings, long stretches of quiet thinking, and conversations with leaders trying to make sense of work that no longer moves the way it once did.

First, thank you to Diana, whose patience, love, and encouragement made the long hours of writing possible. Anyone who has written a book knows that the work rarely happens on a schedule. It shows up early in the morning, late at night, and in moments when the mind refuses to let go of an idea. Your support made the work possible.

I am also grateful to Penny for her thoughtful editorial guidance and her ability to bring clarity and structure to the manuscript. Her work helped sharpen the ideas in these pages and shape them into something readers can engage with clearly.

Many of the observations in this book were shaped by years of conversations with business owners, executives, and operators who were wrestling with the same quiet friction inside their organizations. While none of their stories are told directly here, their experiences shaped the thinking that led to this work.

Finally, I am grateful to God for the clarity, perseverance, and perspective that made this work possible.

If this book helps even a few leaders see their organizations more clearly, then the effort was worthwhile.

Table of Contents

Acknowledgment vii

Introduction 1

PART I – DIAGNOSING STRUCTURAL DRIFT 5

The Early Signals of Structural Drift 7

Leadership as Structural Compensation 13

Structural Misdiagnosis 19

The Architecture of Drift 27

PART II – THE RISK STACK™ 37

The Risk Stack™ 39

The Spaces Between 49

Identity Layer 63

Infrastructure Layer 73

Integration Layer 85

Data Layer 95

Operations Layer 107

Governance Layer 121

Trust Layer 135

What Seeing Requires 149

Reading the Organization 159

About the Author 167

Introduction

The leadership development industry sold you a lie: work harder, communicate better, hold people more accountable, stay closer to the work, and performance will follow. Those actions are all forms of execution. Execution often works, which is why it becomes the default response when strain appears. But there comes a point when execution can no longer improve performance because the structure beneath the work has already begun to fail. Leaders and teams can be executing well while something deeper feels off.

Beneath every organization is a set of structural conditions that shape how authority, accountability, and decisions actually function. I call it the Risk Stack™. The Risk Stack™ is where authority leaks, where decisions lose force, where ownership diffuses, and where trust is borrowed from individuals instead of built into how the organization operates. The Risk Stack™ forms the structure beneath the structure, and this is where drift begins long before the problem becomes visible.

This shift becomes visible inside organizations when work stops moving vertically and begins moving horizontally, yet the structure is never rebuilt to support it. A customer request no longer goes to one person with the authority to resolve it. Instead, it crosses multiple teams, multiple systems, and multiple approval paths before anyone can act.

The same is true for decisions. A decision you make no longer cascades through clear lines of accountability. It ricochets across functions where no one owns the outcome end-to-end. The org chart on your wall still shows a hierarchy, but it no longer describes how work and decisions actually move.

This shift happened because systems, vendors, and teams that once operated independently were integrated into shared workflows. The structure you are leading was designed for vertical authority, but the work now requires horizontal coordination across boundaries that were never built to support it. As coordination becomes manual, decisions stall and accountability fragments. When the system cannot absorb that complexity, people step in, and most of the time that has been you.

You did what you were trained to do. You stepped in, clarified what should have been clear, reconnected teams that should have stayed connected, and made decisions that should have settled several levels below you. Work moved again, the crisis passed, and everyone thanked you for being hands-on and engaged.

Each time you absorbed the gap, the organization learned that nothing else needed to change. When the strain returned, people came back to you, and your continued compensation for structural failure solved each incident in the moment.

This is not theoretical, and the cost is not abstract. When structure stops absorbing complexity, the strain does not disappear. The organization still operates, but it does so by borrowing capacity from the people inside it. Over time, what should have been structural alignment becomes personal effort, and leadership begins to feel heavier than it should. The cost does not stay personal. It spreads into the economics of the business through slower decisions, reduced capacity, and growth that becomes more expensive than it should be. What looks like ordinary pressure is often the hidden operating cost of structure no longer carrying the work.

When structure fails, the weight shifts to people who were never meant to carry it. When leaders burn out or disengage, trust erodes internally and eventually spreads externally. Customers feel it in delayed responses, inconsistent answers, and promises that no longer hold. They experience these failures as service breakdowns or strategic missteps.

You feel this even if you have never named it. Decisions take longer than they should. Meetings exist only to clarify what should already be clear. Work begins to depend on your involvement to move. You feel it at night, when nothing seemed particularly difficult yet everything required more of you than it should have. You feel it when someone praises you for being hands-on in a situation that should never have required your involvement in the first place.

Most frameworks tell you to redraw your org chart, implement better processes, or execute harder. Those approaches treat symptoms rather than structure. The Risk Stack™ shows you where structure stopped working so you can see drift before it shows up as exhaustion, disengagement, or external failure. This is not org design, and it is not execution excellence. It is a structural diagnosis that reveals what those other approaches cannot see.

Once the Risk Stack™ becomes visible, leaders cannot unsee it. Leadership changes, not because you decide to behave differently, but because you can finally see what your effort has been compensating for. You can see where stepping in prevents the organization from learning what it needs to learn, where your presence has become a substitute for alignment that should exist without you, and where responsibility has shifted to you that was never meant to sit at your level.

You may see it in a single day, or even in a single conversation, not months from now after hiring consultants, redesigning your org chart, or launching another initiative that fails for the same underlying reason as the last one. You will see clearly whether the structure is actually working or whether you have been the thing holding it together.

This book will not make leadership easier; it will make it honest. And once you can see what has actually been happening, you will not be able to go back to pretending execution was ever the problem.

PART I

Diagnosing Structural Drift

CHAPTER 1

The Early Signals of Structural Drift

A leader sits in on a conference call that should have taken ten minutes, but it stretches to an hour without a clear cause. At the end, everyone agrees on the decision. No one objects. The call ends, and three weeks later nothing has moved. No one can explain exactly where it stalled, only that it touched several teams along the way. No policy was violated and no person failed. Yet the outcome required more coordination than anyone expected. Moments like this rarely feel significant enough to question the system itself, but they accumulate quietly.

These are the earliest signals of the structural drift that the Risk Stack™ reveals. Most organizations do not show obvious signs when structural problems begin to emerge. They continue to operate. People show up, systems run, and decisions are still made, so little appears different at first. The earliest change is rarely visible in outcomes. The change appears instead in how work moves. Conversations increase, decisions require more clarification, and tasks that used to resolve themselves now require coordination across people who should already be aligned. Simple decisions stretch across multiple conversations that should not be necessary. Progress still happens, but it no longer compounds. Each outcome feels earned through persistence and manual effort rather than carried forward by the structure itself.

This is where the change begins to feel different. The system continues to produce outcomes, but the structure no longer carries the work forward on its own, like a building where the load shifts away from the frame and onto temporary supports. Nothing has collapsed, and from the outside it still looks stable, but more effort is required to hold everything in place.

Early Manifestations of Misalignment

This shift often appears in small, ordinary moments that no one initially recognizes as structural. Someone leaves the company, and six weeks later they still have access to email and internal systems at a publicly traded company. HR processed the termination paperwork, but the manager never triggered the access removal process, IT was never notified that someone had left, and security did not know there was an issue to investigate or resolve. The situation represents a complete failure that occurred in the space between these groups, where no one owned the process end to end.

At first, this feels like variance or an edge case, something that slipped through because timing was off or attention moved elsewhere. Similar gaps then begin appearing in other parts of the organization. A customer issue that should take one conversation now requires three teams and two days before anyone with authority to fix it even knows it exists. A decision everyone agreed to in a weekly meeting still sits unresolved, and no one can explain exactly why or where it stalled. Nothing visibly breaks, so it does not register as failure. Yet the experience stops matching what it should feel like, and the difference becomes harder to dismiss as normal complexity.

This is what structural failure looks like when it first appears. It is not dramatic or loud; the problem appears as tasks falling through gaps no one was responsible for closing, because they crossed boundaries the organization was never designed to support.

What makes these moments dangerous is not their size, but how easily they begin to repeat without anyone naming what they are. A task slips, a decision stalls, a handoff stretches, and each one appears small enough to absorb on its own. But none of them are free. Every repetition adds hidden cost through wasted labor, duplicated attention, and leadership time spent reconnecting what should have held together on its own. Over time, the cost becomes economic. Margin tightens, capacity gets consumed, and the business begins paying more just to keep ordinary work moving.

Execution as Structural Compensation

Because the strain shows up in execution, it is treated like an execution problem. The system pulls attention toward clarifying expectations, refining the process, adding oversight, or layering on more tools in the hope of restoring clarity. These responses seem reasonable, and they often work in the short term. The work continues to move because the organization adapts. But something fundamental has changed beneath the surface, and most leaders do not realize it until they are already exhausted.

When structure effectively supports the work, effort compounds and builds on itself. Progress in one area makes progress in another easier. Decisions create momentum instead of requiring it. Coordination happens naturally rather than through forced intervention, and people trust the system itself to carry work forward without someone having to manually push every piece into place.

When structure drifts out of alignment, effort becomes isolated, and nothing accumulates. Each outcome requires the same renewed force as the last one. Work still gets done, but only when someone compensates for what the structure no longer carries.

This is the point where the cost starts compounding, even if no one has named it yet. The system is no longer carrying momentum forward, so every result has to be earned again through more coordination, more clarification, and more leadership attention than should be necessary. That is not just execution pressure. It is economic drag. The business is now spending more labor and more management time to get the same outcome, which means margin starts getting squeezed long before the problem shows up in obvious ways.

Leadership as Structural Load Bearing

You feel this when you leave work and realize you spent the entire day holding together things that should have stayed aligned on their own. You see it when your calendar fills with meetings devoted to clarifying what should have been clear. You hear it when someone thanks you for stepping in to solve something that should never have required you. And you feel it at night when you are too tired to explain why you are tired, not because the work was strategic but because you spent the day preventing it from drifting apart.

Even when the issue eventually gets resolved, it required your attention, your coordination, and your intervention at a level that should never have been necessary. No one calls this a failure because the outcome was achieved. The situation simply becomes the new normal. Over time, these moments multiply and compound. The organization still produces results, but it does so by continuously drawing down the energy and capacity of its people. This is the point where the strain becomes structural and begins to persist, not only because the work has grown more complex, but because the system has started asking people to do the job it was originally designed to do itself.

These signals appear in familiar ways. You are looped into decisions that once resolved without you. People wait for your presence before moving forward. You carry historical and relational context the system no longer retains. Decisions drift upward even when teams are capable. Your calendar fills with clarification rather than direction. Work accelerates when you intervene and slows when you step away, and the organization begins to feel fragile whenever you are unavailable.

> When leadership presence becomes a prerequisite for flow,
> the architecture has already drifted.

This is where most organizations stop looking. Because the strain surfaces in execution, organizations respond by doing more of what already exists: more coordination, more meetings, more oversight. These responses restore movement in the moment, but the same patterns return. The strain required to achieve the same outcome increases. The system adapts, leaders step in, and nothing appears broken enough to demand a different approach. Compensation becomes normalized because the work still moves. Compensation is not a solution but a signal that something deeper has shifted beneath the surface.

That is what makes early drift dangerous. The organization does not break. It absorbs the cost and keeps moving. Leaders stay closer to the work. Strong employees carry more than they should. Extra coordination becomes normal. And because the business still produces results, no one calls it failure. But doing nothing is not harmless. Each cycle of accepted drift locks more cost into the business, pulls more management attention downward, and uses up more of the capacity that should be fueling growth. The longer it is left alone, the more normal it feels and the more expensive it becomes to correct. By the time it shows up in slower decisions, frustrated clients, margin pressure, or exhausted leadership, it is no longer an early signal. It is already part of how the company operates.

CHAPTER 2

Leadership as Structural Compensation

This chapter shifts the lens toward the experience of leadership from within the role itself. The change does not arrive as a formal transition or a clear turning point. It unfolds through small, reasonable choices that help the work move forward in the moment. Each step feels aligned with responsibility and ownership. Only over time does the pattern become visible, as leadership begins to feel less like guiding direction and more like carrying the weight that structure once held.

The Initial Phase of Structural Compensation

At this stage, nothing about your title changes, but something about the experience of leading does. Decision-making begins to feel less like setting direction and more like stabilizing work that no longer settles on its own.

Leaders increasingly become the people who remembers what was decided, why it mattered, and how teams were supposed to stay aligned because the system no longer carries that understanding forward by itself. They restate decisions, clarify intent, and realign conversations as work crosses boundaries that do not hold context on their own. The organization still produces results, but now it does so because someone is consistently there to keep it moving. This does not register as a problem in the moment but as strong, engaged leadership. Because the approach works, no one questions what the behavior quietly replaces.

Looking back, these changes rarely felt dramatic. They felt responsible. You were included earlier in conversations because your presence helped decisions land faster. Teams paused to check with you, not out of dependence but because experience had taught them that clarity often settled once you were involved. You found yourself repeating decisions and stepping in where alignment used to hold on its own. Each moment seemed reasonable in isolation, even necessary. Only over time did it become clear that your role had expanded beyond leadership into stabilization, and that the system had quietly begun to rely on you in ways it once did not.

A cross-functional project stalls because the marketing team and the product team cannot agree on launch timing. Marketing wants to align with an industry conference three weeks out to capture visibility and press coverage. Product wants another month to include a feature requested by two enterprise customers that could influence renewals. Both positions are reasonable, and neither team has the authority to resolve the trade-off alone. The project sits for days while emails circulate and meetings end without closure. Nothing has failed, yet nothing moves forward.

The leader joins a call to help both teams move forward. They restate the shared goal, weigh the trade-offs, and make the call to move ahead with the conference timing while committing to the enterprise feature in the next release cycle. The decision takes minutes, and the project advances immediately, leaving everyone relieved that clarity returned. The moment feels like strong leadership doing what leadership is supposed to do.

The next time tension appears between the same two teams, they involve the leader earlier. They do not do this because they lack capability but because experience has taught them that progress arrives faster once leadership is present. Over time, decisions that once resolved between teams begin to wait for that presence. The shift happens gradually and rarely feels intentional, but the pattern becomes clear: forward motion increasingly depends on the leader stepping in.

What makes this shift difficult to recognize is that it gets rewarded. The leader appears responsive, trusted, and able to restore movement quickly.

But each time that happens, more of the company's ability to move becomes concentrated in one person. Decisions begin waiting for them. Teams begin relying on them. And the business begins paying for it through slower execution, consumed leadership capacity, and growth constrained by a dependence the structure should never have created.

At that point, the cost is no longer limited to the leader's calendar. The entire business begins to slow down. Decisions that should settle near the work start rising upward before they can move. Teams become more hesitant, not because they lack capability, but because they no longer trust alignment to hold without intervention. That hesitation carries a real cost. Capable people spend more time waiting, checking, and reworking than advancing. Execution slows, capacity gets consumed, and the company begins paying for escalation where structure should have provided flow.

You begin to notice that work waits for you. Work that once moved through shared alignment now waits for direct involvement, and decisions that used to settle between teams begin to stall until someone reconnects them. The organization continues to produce results, but more and more of that progress comes from individual intervention rather than built-in coordination. Over time, the role quietly shifts.

> When leadership shifts from setting direction to stabilizing misalignment, structural drift is already underway.

The Compensation Feedback Loop

At first, this compensation feels temporary and justified. A leader stays close to decisions that matter and joins calls they normally would not attend because the stakes feel high enough to warrant it. They clarify points that should have held on their own but now need their voice behind them to move forward. Each step feels responsible and appropriate, because when they step in, progress resumes and the work moves again.

They begin to notice the pattern and step in earlier, not because anything has already broken, but because experience tells them it will if they do nothing. Questions get answered before they are fully asked, gaps get bridged before they widen, and loops get closed before they open.

Over time, the system adapts. Teams pause longer before moving forward on their own. They check with leadership instead of deciding autonomously. Messages and decisions move upward rather than resolving where they begin. This pattern occurs not out of fear or incompetence but because clarity has learned where to settle and increasingly settles with the leader who has been providing it.

By midweek, the leader's calendar fills with conversations that once resolved without leadership involvement. Nothing is on fire and every discussion is legitimate, yet each meeting prevents a small failure that the system can no longer absorb.

A product manager emails asking which customer request to prioritize. Six months ago, they made that call themselves. Now they wait, because the last time they decided without checking, leadership reversed it three days later, and the work had to be redone. The question is reasonable. The check-in makes sense. But over time, the team has learned that clarity tends to settle with the leader instead of inside the process.

By Friday, the leader is tired in a way that is difficult to name or explain to anyone else. The fatigue does not come from volume or missed deadlines but from feeling spent in a way that seems disproportionate to what actually moved forward. The work advanced and the organization functioned, but most of that movement passed through them. Results were achieved, but they occurred only because someone held the seams together long enough for work to move through.

That is the hidden cost of compensation. Success continues, but it stops proving that the structure is sound. Work moves forward because someone stepped in and carried what the system failed to carry. Over time, that changes how the business runs. Leaders stay too close to decisions. Teams escalate too early. And more of the organization begins to depend on intervention simply to keep ordinary work moving.

Over time, the fatigue is not caused by volume or difficulty, but by becoming the place where clarity settles when the system no longer holds it on its own. Nothing looks broken from the outside, and the organization still moves, decisions still get made, and results still appear. But the weight of alignment has quietly shifted onto the leader.

This kind of fatigue does not remain personal for long because it reflects a deeper shift in how the organization is operating. Work that once moved through shared alignment begins waiting for leadership presence. Decisions that should settle between teams begin rising upward before they can move. More of the company's ability to maintain momentum becomes concentrated in one person. That is where the cost begins to spread. Leadership time gets pulled into work that should never have required it. Execution slows as more decisions wait for intervention, and the company becomes increasingly dependent on expensive attention simply to produce ordinary results.

> When leadership presence becomes necessary for alignment, structure is no longer doing its job.

CHAPTER 3

Structural Misdiagnosis

This chapter widens the lens, moving away from the individual leader toward how organizations interpret what is happening. When work begins to feel heavier and movement depends more on intervention than on structure, organizations do not assume the system has changed. They return to what they were taught to do, focusing on execution, adding tools, and refining the process in an effort to restore momentum. These responses feel reasonable because the strain is most visible in execution, even when the real shift began somewhere deeper.

The Diagnostic Trap

When work stops moving cleanly through the organization, leaders do not invent a new response. They return to what they were taught to do: working harder, communicating more, adding structure, and staying closer to the work. Execution becomes the focus not because leaders misunderstand their role, but because execution is where problems become visible. This is where the mistake happens, because what is visible is not always the cause of the problem.

Execution is where structural misalignment becomes visible, but it is not where it begins. By the time work feels heavy at the execution layer, the real shift has already taken place somewhere else.

This is not unique to organizations. It is how people respond to problems everywhere. We address issues where they become visible rather than where they actually begin. The symptom appears at the point of impact, so that is where we apply effort. We treat what we can measure and act on immediately, while the real cause sits beneath the work in places we have not been trained to examine or do not fully own. Organizations solve the wrong problem not because leaders are careless, but because the real issue rarely announces itself in a place that feels clear or controllable. This dynamic becomes clear in practice.

A sales team builds its process around a modern CRM system. Opportunities are tracked, notes are thorough, and forecasts stay up to date. When a deal closes, the record is marked complete and handed to operations. Inside the sales process, the work is finished and the handoff looks clean.

Operations receives the handoff and realizes the work does not translate the way sales expected. Nothing is missing from the transfer, but sales and operations are working from different definitions of what counts as standard work. What sales considered routine delivery, operations sees as custom work that will require additional resources and timeline adjustments. Flexibility promised during the sale now looks like scope that was never formally defined. No one is acting in bad faith or failing to do their job. Each team is operating within its own system and following the process it was given.

The deal stalls, and leadership steps in to help move it forward. They review the CRM, walk through the handoff, and read the notes sales provided alongside the questions coming from operations. Nothing appears broken inside either team's process, so attention turns to execution. Leaders look for ways to tighten the handoff, add clarity, and prevent the problem from happening again.

To fix it, leaders add a meeting to review handoffs more carefully, create a checklist to ensure nothing gets missed, add fields to the CRM to capture more detail up front, and assign someone to own the transition between sales and ops. The deal eventually moves forward through intervention rather than flow, and the organization believes it solved the problem because execution improved and movement returned.

But nothing about the structure changed. Work still moved horizontally from sales to operations across a boundary that depended on alignment the organization never explicitly established. The structure assumed alignment between two teams that operate with different definitions, different incentives, and different measures of success. When that assumption failed, the strain showed up in execution, so execution is what got fixed.

This is the diagnostic trap. The problem becomes visible in execution, so execution is where the organization applies effort, even when the cause sits elsewhere. The improvements are real, and they produce short-term stability, but they do not address why the boundary between sales and ops cannot transfer work cleanly. The next time work crosses that same boundary, the same pattern returns. Over time, compensation becomes the operating model. Handoffs require supervision, and movement depends on someone manually connecting work that the structure should have carried on its own.

The cost of this mistake is not only that the problem returns. The business keeps paying to manage the same failure in different forms. Time, money, and leadership attention are directed toward tightening execution where the strain appears, while the boundary beneath the work continues producing the same friction. Each fix looks responsible. Each intervention provides enough relief to justify the next one. But over time the organization becomes more supervised, more dependent on escalation, and more expensive to run because ordinary work no longer moves cleanly on its own.

> When structural misalignment is treated as an execution issue, the organization works harder at the wrong one.

Tools as Structural Substitutes

Once execution becomes framed as the problem, the range of acceptable responses narrows quickly. The organization wants reliability restored without slowing momentum or disrupting what is already working. Solutions need to fit inside existing rhythms and existing budgets without requiring anyone to stop and redesign how the business actually operates. Tools meet that need perfectly because they restore reliability without forcing reconsideration of the underlying structure. Dashboards promise visibility, CRMs promise control, and workflow systems promise consistency. Each one allows leaders to respond to the strain without asking harder questions about whether the structure beneath the work still carries it.

Tools also fit naturally with how ownership is already distributed across the organization. Sales owns the CRM, ops owns the workflow tools, and finance owns the reporting layer. When execution starts to feel heavier, the natural instinct is to improve the system that is owned and controlled locally. It feels responsible to fix what sits inside your domain rather than to question what lives between domains or across boundaries you do not directly control. This is how organizations begin addressing symptoms locally while the structural source of strain remains untouched.

Every tool reveals only the portion of the work it was designed to measure. A CRM reflects sales activity, a workflow system enforces operational steps, and a dashboard aggregates metrics drawn from individual systems. None of them are built to see what happens when work leaves one environment and enters another, where assumptions are tested, ownership shifts, and coordination must be rebuilt in motion. Those transitions do not belong to a single tool, yet they are precisely where execution breaks down and where the real structural strain lives.

Despite this, organizations keep adding tools because doing so feels like progress. Tools create an appearance of order and give leaders something to implement, measure, and point to when asked what is being done about the problem. Redesigning structure requires stepping back, revisiting assumptions that have been in place for years, and confronting ambiguity that has often been avoided because it was easier to work around it than to resolve it. Tools allow leaders to stay in motion while deferring that deeper work. Technology did not create the structural shift, but it made it livable.

That is why the pattern becomes so costly. The organization sees more movement and assumes progress is being made, even while the underlying condition remains unchanged. More systems are added, more fields are completed, more dashboards are reviewed, and more activity becomes visible. But visibility is not the same as alignment. In many cases the business simply becomes heavier. Complexity increases, maintenance expands, and leaders take on more administrative load just to keep ordinary work moving. The company appears more controlled while becoming harder to align and more expensive to operate.

Once work went horizontal, organizations added technology instead of rebuilding structure. CRMs became places where decisions stalled because no one owned them end to end. Workflow tools became parking lots for work no one wanted to assign clearly. Instead of redesigning how work moved through the organization, technology gave the work somewhere to live. Nothing had to be resolved; the work only had to be tracked.

The tools did what they were designed to do, making broken structures feel manageable and allowing organizations to continue operating without addressing what was broken underneath. Companies spend millions on systems that are supposed to solve the problem but often make the dysfunction easier to live with. Technology did not fix the underlying structure; it made it possible to keep operating without addressing what was actually broken. And because nothing fundamental changed, the weight did not disappear; it relocated.

Over time, this pattern of solving structural strain with tools compounds in ways that are difficult to reverse. Each new tool improves local effectiveness while increasing overall complexity across the organization. Teams adapt to the tool rather than to the work itself. Visibility increases, but clarity does not follow. The organization becomes better at managing activity while remaining poorly aligned around outcomes. Because tools are measurable, visible, and easy to implement without disrupting current operations, organizations treat them as the default response every time execution starts to feel strained. The organization learns that when execution feels unreliable, the responsible move is to add more tools rather than examine the structure beneath the work.

This is one of the most expensive forms of organizational drift because it can persist for years while being mistaken for maturity. Teams stay busy, systems remain active, and reports continue to show movement, yet the business keeps getting heavier underneath. More effort is required to produce the same results. More coordination is needed to preserve client confidence. More senior time is consumed resolving issues that should have settled lower in the system. The company does not appear stalled. It appears disciplined. But much of that discipline is simply compensation turned into routine.

The Compounding Cost of Misdiagnosis

This diagnostic error does not stay contained inside the organization. The strain that starts at the interface between teams eventually surfaces beyond the organization itself. Clients feel it first, as responses take longer, answers feel inconsistent, and handoffs require them to repeat context that should have moved internally. Trust erodes quietly, revenue follows, sales cycles lengthen, renewals require more justification, and growth slows not because demand disappears but because the organization cannot move work cleanly once it secures it. Leaders rarely diagnose the slowdown as structural. It is attributed to execution challenges or market pressure instead.

The first signal rarely appears on the balance sheet. It shows up in stretched timelines, rising rework, and senior leaders pulled into escalations that should not require them. Coordination increases, effort multiplies, and discounts smooth over problems that should never have occurred. The business looks busy, but margins tighten and pressure increases without a clear source anyone can isolate and correct.

Eventually growth becomes both a target and a threat. Each new client increases pressure on already strained boundaries. Each new product adds complexity across interfaces the organization was never designed to carry. Small disruptions cascade more easily, recovery takes longer, and resilience declines because intervention has replaced structure.

The pattern becomes a structural cost that accumulates when organizations solve the wrong problem. It appears not as a single dramatic failure but as compounding inefficiencies, rising costs without clear explanation, and growth that feels harder to sustain than it should. Leaders see margin pressure, client strain, and execution challenges.

What leaders often do not see is that these are no longer separate problems. They are the same structural failure appearing in different places. By the time margins tighten, client trust begins to slip, and senior leaders are pulled into routine friction, the business is no longer paying in inconvenience. It is paying in slower growth, weaker accountability, higher operating costs, and leadership time that never reaches the future because it keeps getting spent holding the present together.

Work is moving through a structure that was never designed to carry it.

CHAPTER 4

The Architecture of Drift

This chapter moves beneath the instinct to fix execution and instead examines the architecture itself. Drift is not a failure of execution or discipline; it is a structural condition that forms gradually as the organization's design falls out of alignment with how work actually moves. To understand why compensation becomes necessary and why execution becomes the wrong diagnosis, we must first define architectural drift clearly and examine how it forms.

Architectural Drift Defined

Most organizations treat problems as events: a bad decision, a missed target, a market shift that changed everything. They search for a moment they can name and correct. But some structural conditions develop without a clear starting point or visible boundary. They are not tied to a single decision or failure, and because of that, they are rarely addressed at their source.

The condition is drift, more specifically architectural drift, which is the most common structural failure in modern organizations. Most leaders never learn to see the problem because the failure does not appear as a mistake that can be traced to a single decision or person. Drift forms gradually as the organization's structure stops matching how work actually moves. There is no starting line, no inflection point, and no single choice that creates it. Roles evolve to meet new demands, systems expand to absorb greater complexity, vendors shift as the business grows, and workflows adapt to new realities.

Each adjustment happens in isolation while the architecture meant to hold them together remains largely unchanged. The organization continues to function and produce results, but resistance quietly increases. Architectural drift becomes visible through four structural dimensions:

- Authority becomes unclear when the people who need to make decisions no longer hold the right to make them.

- Ownership becomes displaced when responsibility for outcomes shifts to people or teams who were never designed to carry it.

- Accountability weakens when results depend on coordination between groups that have no shared way to measure success or resolve conflict.

- Trust erodes when the organization can no longer rely on its systems to move work forward, and confidence concentrates in individuals instead of the structure itself.

These four dimensions are signals of a single structural mismatch. When authority, ownership, accountability, and trust begin to drift, the architecture is no longer aligned with how work actually moves.

Drift does not begin with failure. It forms when work starts moving in ways the structure was never designed to carry. Decisions that once stayed inside a single function begin crossing multiple teams, customer requests expand beyond their original owners, and processes that once felt straightforward begin depending on assumptions that are no longer shared. The org chart still shows clean lines, but the work no longer follows them. It moves horizontally across boundaries the architecture was never meant to support.

Over time, the structure remains intact on paper while the reality beneath it shifts. Authority transfers informally, responsibility shifts without redesign, information flows around the system rather than through it, and trust relocates from structure to individuals. The organization keeps operating, but the gap between design and reality widens until coordination feels heavier than the work itself. This is not a failure of effort or execution but the accumulated effect of architectural drift.

Consider a professional services firm that expands its offerings over time to meet client demand. Each service line launches with capable people and its own tools and processes. The original structure was designed when the firm had only a few core services, and as the business grows that structure is never redesigned to accommodate what has changed. The firm adapts around it instead. Delivery teams coordinate informally across service lines, leaders step in to resolve conflicts between practices, and clients get reassured when handoffs feel uneven. The work gets done and revenue continues to grow, but something fundamental shifts beneath the surface.

A client request that once moved cleanly through one team now crosses multiple service lines before anyone knows who owns the outcome. Decisions slow as people reconstruct scope and responsibility that used to be obvious. Timelines stretch, not because individuals are moving slowly, but because alignment has to be rebuilt every time work moves across a boundary. Senior leaders become the bridge that keeps routine situations moving.

The firm does not experience this as failure. Growth continues, new services launch, and clients stay. The cost hides inside the effort required to maintain flow. What structure once handled automatically now depends on people who coordinate, translate, and step in to close gaps the architecture should have closed on its own. Over time the structure still exists on paper, but it no longer carries the work the way it once did. No one calls this drift. They call it growth, complexity, or the price of operating at scale.

That is what makes drift so dangerous. Once added weight is accepted as the normal cost of growth, the organization stops seeing it as a warning. Extra coordination begins to feel justified. Escalation begins to look disciplined. Leaders getting pulled into routine decisions begins to look like leadership. From that point forward, the business no longer corrects the misalignment; it builds around it. The company is no longer just carrying drift structurally. It is paying for it economically through slower throughput, higher labor costs, weaker margins, and growth that becomes more expensive than it should be.

Not all weight represents drift, because organizations that expand their scope carry coordination costs proportional to what they have taken on. Drift is not the presence of weight but weight the work did not earn. When friction scales with scope, the right response is capability. When friction scales with time, the only response is realignment. Confuse the two and organizations invest years building sophistication to compensate for architecture that has quietly fallen behind.

Each adjustment solves a real problem, and each workaround makes sense in the moment. Over time those adjustments reshape how work moves until effort becomes the primary driver of progress instead of structure carrying momentum forward. No one plans for this shift. It happens because work keeps evolving and the organization keeps adapting to keep pace.

Drift lives in the spaces between things rather than inside them. It forms where responsibility should transfer but does not, where teams operate from different assumptions, where systems require manual translation, and where partnerships were never designed to preserve context or maintain momentum.

No function owns those spaces and no system measures their health. Drift remains invisible even as its effects ripple across the organization. The weight is felt long before the source becomes clear.

By the time the source finally becomes visible, the cost has usually spread far beyond where the mismatch began. Teams have adjusted around it. Leaders have reorganized their time to absorb it. Clients begin experiencing a slower, heavier version of the business without anyone naming why. What began as structural misalignment has become part of how the company operates. The organization is no longer just carrying drift. It is paying for it through slower movement, reduced capacity, and margin that keeps getting consumed by friction no one intended to build into the work.

Eventually misalignment becomes the baseline everyone accepts as normal. Coordination replaces natural momentum, interpretation replaces clarity, and leaders carry more responsibility not because their role requires it but because the structure beneath them no longer does. The heaviness that emerges is neither random nor personal but the signal of an architecture that has quietly drifted out of alignment with the work it was meant to support.

Drift as Structural Diagnosis

Drift is not the same as organizational dysfunction, poor execution, or resistance to change, which are symptoms of the structural condition that produces them.

Systems thinking reminds you that everything is connected and that changes ripple across the organization. That is true, but it does not tell you where alignment failed or how to identify the point where structure stopped supporting how work actually moves. Drift does.

Org design redraws boxes, reporting lines, and roles in the hope that work will flow differently. But drift explains why reorgs often fail. The issue is not the boxes themselves. It is that work now moves across them in ways the architecture was never designed to carry.

Change management treats transformation as an execution challenge. It focuses on communication, buy-in, training, and adoption. But drift is not an adoption problem. It is a structural mismatch. You cannot execute your way out of drift because execution is where drift becomes visible, not where it begins.

Drift is structural diagnosis, not process improvement or behavior change. It reveals where authority, ownership, accountability, and trust have migrated away from where they were meant to rest. Until you can see drift as a structural condition, every solution will treat symptoms while the architecture continues to deteriorate. The Formation of Drift Drift does not require a decision or a moment of failure to begin. It forms through accumulation, not intention. The organization adapts to real constraints, solves real problems, and responds to real pressure. A new team gets added to handle complexity.

A workflow adjusts to accommodate an unusual request. A vendor fills a capacity gap. An approval step gets introduced after an avoidable error. Each response is reasonable on its own.

The problem is not the adjustment. It is that the architecture connecting these adjustments is never revisited. The org chart remains static while work moves differently. Roles stay defined as they were while responsibility shifts to wherever the work actually lands. Systems remain configured for processes that no longer reflect how decisions are made. The structure stands still while everything beneath it evolves.

Early friction rarely feels threatening because it appears as ordinary complexity. Dependencies require coordination, handoffs need clarification, and delays call for follow-up, yet each instance appears manageable on its own. The responsible response is to compensate, and compensation succeeds. Work continues to move forward, which makes it easy to assume that nothing fundamental has shifted beneath the surface.

Over time, however, what begins as temporary adjustment gradually becomes permanent. Additional steps are layered into the process, oversight expands, and communication increases until the system feels more careful and deliberate from the inside. These adaptations can resemble maturity. What is less visible is that the formal structure is no longer carrying the work as it once did; instead, people are absorbing the strain that design previously contained.

As this pattern settles into normalcy, new employees inherit the adapted version of the system rather than the one originally intended. They are trained to navigate friction instead of questioning its presence, and they learn to anticipate gaps and absorb misalignment before it spreads. Their competence keeps the organization functioning, but it also reduces the urgency to redesign what no longer fits, because the system appears stable so long as capable people continue compensating for its weaknesses.

Eventually, survival begins to justify itself. Redesign feels risky when revenue is still flowing and clients are still being served, and pausing to examine how work truly moves can seem more disruptive than continuing to adjust. Drift appears safer than intervention because continuation feels less dangerous than interruption. The weight continues to increase, yet it is accepted as the cost of operating at scale rather than recognized as evidence of structural misalignment.

But drift does not stay contained. The longer it remains unaddressed, the more of the organization adapts around it. Workarounds harden. Extra coordination becomes part of the job. More people spend time compensating for something the structure should have resolved. What once felt easier to leave alone becomes more expensive to unwind later because the misalignment spreads into roles, routines, and the normal movement of the business.

This is how drift persists. It does not require defense; it requires only that it remain unnamed. As long as attention stays fixed on execution, the architecture beneath it goes unexamined, and by the time the mismatch becomes visible, the workaround has hardened into the system itself, leaving little memory of what it once replaced.

The Surface Manifestations of Drift

Drift disguises itself as problems organizations are trained to solve. When work slows, it appears to be an execution issue. When questions repeat, it looks like a communication breakdown. When progress requires additional approvals, it seems like a process failure. Leaders respond rationally by tightening accountability, adding meetings, and introducing more controls. Improvement follows, but it does not last.

The issue is structural misalignment rather than effort, discipline, or communication. Drift lives beneath behavior, in the architecture that governs how decisions, responsibility, and information move once they leave the room where they were created. Because strain is most visible at the surface, organizations continue treating symptoms while the structure producing them remains untouched.

The Structural Cost of Drift

Drift does not just make work harder. It reshapes the organization in ways that are increasingly difficult to reverse.

When authority drifts away from the place where decisions need to be made, speed and confidence disappear. Decisions begin to stall, opportunities pass more easily, and competitors move faster because they are not carrying the same structural weight. When ownership drifts, accountability dissolves, and performance becomes unpredictable. When accountability spans teams without a shared measure of success, trust erodes. Collaboration turns into negotiation, and alignment turns political. The organization continues to function, but it fractures internally.

As trust migrates from structure to individuals, the organization grows fragile. It depends on specific people holding things together. When they leave or burn out, the strain becomes visible. Confidence erodes quietly and revenue follows. Growth slows not because demand disappears, but because the organization cannot move work cleanly after securing it. Drift does not announce itself as a crisis, but it steadily creates the conditions for one.

The cost, however, is not only external or financial. It is also experiential. It is felt inside the organization as weight. Most leaders assume weight belongs where they feel it most. If decisions feel heavy, judgment must be off. If execution feels slow, discipline must be slipping. If coordination takes longer than before, people must work harder or communicate better. In that interpretation, weight becomes a performance problem.

> Weight is not a performance problem.
> It is structural information.

Weight accumulates where structure has stopped carrying the work it was designed to carry. It shows up where work crosses unsupported boundaries, responsibility transfers without clarity, and meaning thins as it moves through the system. When weight is misread as effort instead of information, leaders begin compensating for architecture they can no longer see. Over time, that compensation turns capable organizations into exhausting ones.

Effort can move work forward, but it cannot make it lighter. If the same outcomes require increasing force over time, something structural has shifted. Weight is not judgment; weight is signal. It indicates that force is being applied where the structure should have been carrying load.

Read correctly, that signal changes the diagnosis. Read incorrectly, it keeps the organization pushing harder where structure has already stopped carrying the work. From there the cost accelerates. Delays spread, leadership time is consumed by problems that should have settled lower in the system, and capable people spend more of their effort holding things together instead of moving them forward. The business still functions, but at a higher cost, with less capacity, and with growth that becomes harder to sustain than it should be.

Until drift is recognized, effort will continue compensating for structure, and weight will keep accumulating where it does not belong. The question is no longer how to push harder. It is where the architecture stopped supporting the work and why.

The Risk Stack™

Every organization has a stack beneath its visible systems, yet we name stacks only for the tools that sit on top of it: tech stack, marketing stack, data stack, operations stack. We obsess over the systems that move work, measure activity, and track performance. What we have never named is the structural stack that carries weight when those systems stop working, and in the absence of that structure, leaders carry it instead.

The Risk Stack™ is the structural layer where authority holds or leaks, ownership transfers cleanly or diffuses, accountability aligns or fragments, and trust either stabilizes the system or concentrates in individuals. It sits beneath org charts, processes, and technology. It determines whether work moves because structure carries it or because people compensate for what structure no longer supports.

I call this structural lens the Risk Stack™ not because it creates risk, but because it reveals where risk is already being carried. It shows where load has settled in places it was never meant to rest. The work that follows is not about behavior, process, or additional tools. It is about examining this structural layer and redesigning how it carries weight.

> The Risk Stack™ makes structural drift visible.

PART II:
· · · · · · ·

The Risk Stack™

CHAPTER 5

The Risk Stack™

This chapter turns to where drift actually forms and how it travels through the organization. Drift does not distribute randomly but instead forms in specific structural layers, travels along predictable paths, and eventually surfaces where the system can no longer absorb it quietly. To understand why the same strain appears in the same places, we must examine the underlying stack through which modern organizations already operate. Beneath every organization is the structure where authority fragments, ownership shifts without redesign, and trust migrates from architecture to individuals. That structure is the Risk Stack™.

The Risk Stack™ Defined

The Risk Stack™ is not a framework layered on top of an organization, and it is not an overlay or diagnostic tool. It is the underlying structure through which modern organizations already operate, whether they recognize it or not. It remained unnamed not because it did not exist, but because the mental models used to understand organizations lagged behind how organizations themselves evolved. When work was mostly contained within functions, that gap was manageable. Once work became distributed across systems, vendors, platforms, and partners, the distance between reality and the way leaders were taught to interpret it became impossible to ignore.

Organizations today are assembled environments rather than deliberately designed ones. Systems are adopted rather than built, vendors are integrated rather than owned, and platforms evolve independently of the businesses that rely on them. A decision made in one meeting can trigger consequences across infrastructure, contracts, permissions, workflows, and third-party systems that no one in the room can fully see. What appears to be a single organization from the outside is, in practice, a network of internal and external dependencies that cannot be controlled from any single point.

Yet most organizations are still interpreted as if they were self-contained machines, where problems originate where they appear and accountability is assigned based on role rather than influence. When outcomes disappoint, the reflex is to intervene locally and apply pressure where pain is visible. Sometimes improvement follows, but more often the strain simply relocates. What stabilizes in one place destabilizes in another. The same issues resurface under different names, in different departments, with different people involved.

This pattern is structural, not accidental. The issue is not that organizations lack structure, but that the structure shaping outcomes is rarely the one leaders are trained to examine.

Without a structural model that accounts for this, leaders reason from the surface inward. They respond to what is visible and intervene where accountability appears to reside. Over time, structural clarity decreases while leadership effort increases. Presence replaces design and judgment substitutes for architecture. The organization continues to function, but only through continuous correction routed through people. The The Risk Stack™ exists to make that architecture visible.

> The Risk Stack™ is not something you add. It is the structure your organization is already operating through, whether you name it or not.

The Seven Layers of the Risk Stack™

The Risk Stack™ is composed of seven layers. These are neither departments nor functions. They are domains of reality that govern how work becomes possible, how it moves, how it is measured, how it is authorized, and how it is trusted. They are always present, even when unnamed. The confusion in most organizations is not that structure is missing, but that it is operating invisibly, which makes cause and effect feel disconnected. The structure becomes visible through the following layers:

1. **Identity**: Who can access systems and act within them. It governs credentials, permissions, and the operational authority to execute work.

2. **Infrastructure**: The systems, platforms, vendors, and technical foundations that make work physically possible.

3. **Integration**: How systems, teams, and external dependencies connect, and whether those connections preserve meaning as work moves between them.

4. **Data**: The information the organization relies on to make decisions, and whether that information is accurate, accessible, and interpreted consistently.

5. **Operations**: How work actually gets done, the processes that govern execution, and whether those processes align with how work needs to move.

6. **Governance**: Where decision rights sit and who holds authority over outcomes. It governs how trade-offs are resolved, how priorities are set, and how consequence is assigned when work crosses boundaries.

7. **Trust**: Whether the organization can rely on its systems and structure to carry work forward, or whether trust must be borrowed from individuals.

These layers sit on top of each other in a sequential relationship: identity enables infrastructure, infrastructure enables integration, integration enables data, data enables operations, operations enable governance, and governance ultimately builds or erodes trust. The Risk Stack™ is best visualized as a layered structure in which each domain supports the one above it.

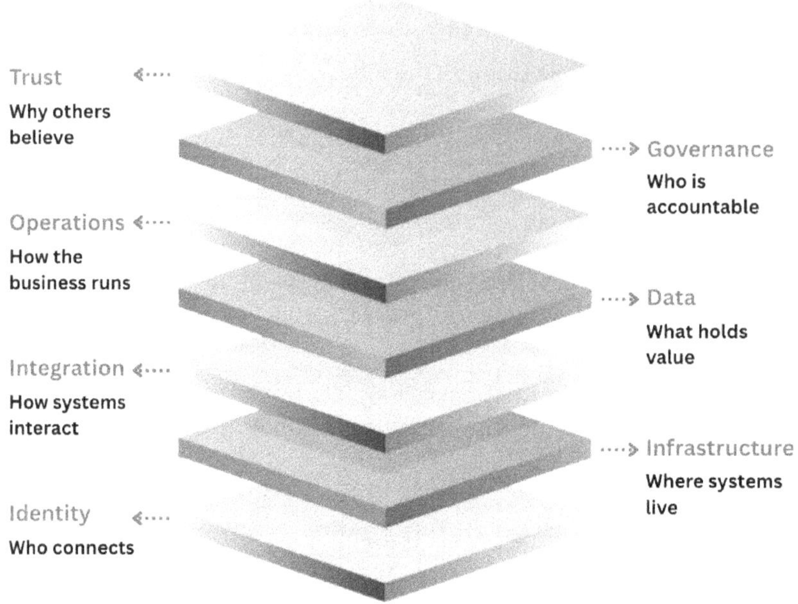

When the layers are aligned, work moves cleanly, decisions hold, and outcomes are predictable. When alignment breaks at any layer, strain forms and does not remain contained. Work moves downward toward execution, but failure travels upward until it reaches a layer that can absorb it or a person who must compensate for it.

Problems form in one layer but surface in another. A stalled decision may not be a governance issue but an identity failure about who is authorized to act. A system failure may not be infrastructure but integration that failed to preserve context. Revenue may slow not because operations weakened, but because trust eroded when the structure could no longer carry what was promised.

What feels like chaos is often misalignment moving through layers that were never designed to function as a coherent system.

How Problems Travel Through the Risk Stack™

To understand how the Risk Stack™ works in practice, consider what happens inside a company rolling out a new enterprise product across multiple regions. The product itself is sound, the strategy is clear, and leadership alignment is strong. Sales closes deals confidently, marketing drives demand, and operations is staffed and trained. On paper everything is ready, and the first customers onboard smoothly, until friction begins to appear in unexpected places.

A contract signed by sales triggers provisioning delays because system permissions conflict with regional infrastructure requirements. Sales did nothing wrong; the issue was not execution, but misalignment between identity and infrastructure. The structure never defined how regional access constraints should be reconciled once commitments were made, so the provisioning team escalates to leadership for resolution. Leadership intervenes manually, the customer is onboarded, and the organization moves on.

Two weeks later support receives tickets they cannot resolve because access is limited by security policies no one updated when the product launched. Support does not lack capability, but it lacks the infrastructure access required to perform its work. The issue is not at the operations layer where the symptom appeared. The issue is at the infrastructure layer where systems were never configured to support the work support was hired to do. The issue is resolved through a manual exception rather than structural alignment.

A month later finance blocks invoicing because customer records do not match compliance requirements in a third-party system. The data exists, but it does not flow cleanly from the CRM to the billing platform to the compliance system. Each system holds a piece of the truth but no single system holds the complete picture. The problem is not that finance is failing to do its job. The problem is that integration was never designed to preserve meaning as data moves from one system to another. The records are manually reconciled and the invoice goes out.

Nothing is broken but nothing moves cleanly. The same issues recur with every new customer. Leaders find themselves pulled deeper into operational detail even though the strategy, product, and market remain unchanged. What has changed is that work is now moving across multiple layers of dependency that were never aligned to carry it end to end.

This sequence illustrates the Risk Stack™ in motion. The problem started at identity, where no one clearly owned who could authorize access across regions. That failure cascaded to infrastructure, where systems were not configured to support the work, and then to integration, where data could not move cleanly between systems. It eventually surfaced at operations, where support could not resolve tickets and finance could not process invoices. From there the weight reached governance, where leadership had to make decisions that should have been resolved structurally. As exceptions accumulated, trust in the system weakened and reliance on leadership increased.

By the time leadership felt the strain, the problem had already traveled through five layers of the Risk Stack™. What looked like an execution problem at the operations layer was actually a structural failure that started at identity. Fixing execution, adding process, or training the teams would not have solved it. The only thing that could have solved it was seeing where the problem actually started and aligning the layers so they could carry the work on their own.

Problems do not remain where they begin. They surface where they can no longer be absorbed.

Seeing the Risk Stack™

Once the Risk Stack™ becomes visible, something fundamental shifts in how you understand your organization. What once felt chaotic begins to look structured, and what felt personal begins to feel located. The weight you have been carrying no longer appears as a failure of effort or capability, but as the predictable result of structural layers that have drifted out of alignment with how work actually moves.

You have been fixing problems at the point of impact, but the Risk Stack™ reveals the point of origin.

This distinction changes how the organization is understood, because when problems are addressed at the point of impact, symptoms improve temporarily while the source remains active beneath the surface. The strain does not disappear but instead shifts elsewhere. It emerges in another part of the organization because the underlying misalignment continues to produce the same friction. Intervention restores stability for a time, but without structural correction the pattern inevitably returns.

This is why leadership has become exhausting in otherwise capable organizations. Leaders are not confronting new categories of problems. They are encountering recurring structural failures that surface in different places as work crosses the same misaligned boundaries. Each intervention stabilizes visible outcomes while the architecture beneath them continues to drift, increasing effort even as structural clarity decreases, until presence substitutes for design and judgment replaces alignment. The organization continues to move, but it does so through ongoing correction rather than structural coherence.

The cycle is structural, not random. The Risk Stack™ interrupts that cycle by revealing where problems actually form.

Once this becomes visible, the questions change. When a decision stalls, the assumption is no longer that execution failed. Instead, you examine whether governance is clear about authority, whether data is reaching the right people in a usable form, or whether identity was ever aligned on who had the right to act. When operations feel heavy, the response is no longer to add process automatically, but to examine whether infrastructure truly supports the work, whether integration preserves meaning as work moves between systems, and whether operations is compensating for failures that began several layers below where strain became visible.

This is what distinguishes the Risk Stack™ from other frameworks. Systems thinking acknowledges interconnection but does not specify where alignment has broken. Organizational redesign adjusts reporting lines without addressing why work flows across them in unstable ways. Change management treats transformation as an execution challenge even though execution is the layer where structural failure becomes visible, not where it originates.

The Risk Stack™ provides structural clarity by revealing where problems form, how they travel, and why they consistently surface in the same locations. It does not require an immediate reorganization or another initiative layered on top of the existing system. It requires learning to see the structure that is already operating and recognizing where it has drifted out of alignment with how work actually moves.

With that clarity, compensation becomes optional rather than reflexive. You can distinguish between problems that require direct intervention and those that require structural realignment. You can recognize when stepping in preserves progress and when it prevents the organization from confronting misalignment that must be addressed. This does not make leadership easier, but it does make it honest.

The Transition Forward

At some point in reading this, you likely stopped thinking about organizations in general and began seeing your own. You recognized the initiatives that never fully land, the decisions that require follow-up long after they should have taken hold, the issues that arrive escalated because no one could clearly own them earlier, and the quiet reliance on a handful of people who know how things actually move. These patterns are not accidental or personal, but structural. Once that realization settles, the question changes: the issue is no longer why this keeps happening, but where it is forming.

The Risk Stack™ exists to answer that question in practical terms. It does not require a six-month transformation effort, a reorganization, or another initiative layered on top of an already strained system. It requires learning to see the structure that is carrying work and recognizing whether it is doing so by design or by compensation. When you see it clearly, you can determine whether the system is functioning as designed or whether momentum depends primarily on your continued intervention.

What comes next is not about implementing the Risk Stack™. It is about examining the structure through which your organization is already operating, layer by layer, so you can see where drift is forming and why it continues to surface in the same locations.

This examination requires a different kind of attention, one that involves looking at the spaces between roles, systems, and decisions where responsibility transfers and meaning either holds or thins. It involves recognizing that most recurring problems do not originate inside the boxes on an organizational chart, but in the connections between them that were never designed to carry sustained load.

At this point, the analysis deepens, and the descent is not into chaos or disorder but into clarity. It is a movement toward the structure that has been present all along, shaping outcomes beneath the surface of what appeared to be isolated execution failures.

When organizations behave with this level of consistency, there is always structure beneath the behavior. The Risk Stack™ provides language for that structure and a way to examine it deliberately, layer by layer, so the architecture influencing your results can finally be understood.

> Once that architecture becomes visible, it becomes difficult to attribute recurring strain to execution alone.

CHAPTER 6

The Spaces Between

This chapter shifts the focus from the layers themselves to what happens as work moves between them. Modern organizations no longer operate vertically inside clean boundaries. Work moves horizontally across functions, systems, vendors, and decisions, and every crossing is a place where authority can blur, context can thin, and ownership can fragment. To understand why capable organizations feel heavier than they should, we have to examine the spaces between the layers where structure stops carrying weight and people begin.

The Horizontal Shift

The Risk Stack™ shows you the layers through which modern organizations operate: identity, infrastructure, integration, data, operations, governance, and trust. These are the domains that govern how work becomes possible, how it moves, how it is measured, and whether it can be trusted to carry forward on its own. When these layers are aligned, the organization feels coherent and work flows cleanly. When they drift out of alignment, strain begins to form and weight migrates upward until it lands on someone who can carry it. What most leaders miss is where the problem actually lives.

> Problems live in the crossings, not in the components.

Here is what the shift from vertical to horizontal actually means in practice. A sales team closes a deal with a new enterprise customer. The contract requires integration with the customer's existing systems, custom reporting dashboards, and specific data governance controls that were not part of the standard package. In a vertically structured organization, this request would have a clear owner who had the authority to approve the customization, allocate resources, and ensure delivery. The decision would move up if needed, get resolved, and move back down with clarity.

But work does not move that way anymore. The sales leader does not have authority over engineering priorities, so they escalate to the VP of Sales. Engineering cannot commit without understanding technical requirements, which brings in solutions architecture. The integration requires access controls under security's domain and data flows that the data team must evaluate for compliance, pulling in legal and finance before anyone can confirm the work is justified.

The work has moved horizontally across six functions before anyone can say yes or no. Each handoff makes sense on its own, and each team is doing exactly what it is supposed to do, but no single person owns the outcome end to end, and no single layer of authority can resolve it without coordinating across all the others. The work is sitting in the spaces between functions, waiting for someone to manually shepherd it through.

This is not a failure of any individual or team. This is what horizontal work looks like, and the structures most organizations operate with were never designed to support it. Authority still sits vertically within functions, but the work requires horizontal movement across them. That mismatch is where the weight lives, and it does not resolve itself. Someone has to carry it.

A decision is made in a meeting on Monday morning. The direction is clear, the tradeoffs were debated, the room is aligned, and everyone leaves nodding. There is even a slide that captures the conclusion in clean and confident language. By any traditional measure, the work of leadership is done, governance worked, and the decision was made, documented, and communicated.

By Wednesday, the questions begin, not as objections or resistance, but as clarifications. One team asks whether the decision applies to existing clients or only new ones. Another asks how it interacts with a tool they already rely on. A third flags that a vendor contract may limit what was just agreed to. None of this came up in the meeting, and none of it feels unreasonable. The questions are answered quickly and assumed to be normal friction of execution.

By Friday the decision no longer looks the same. It has split into versions. The intent is still there but the shape has changed as it moved. Each team is operating on a slightly different understanding of what was decided. The same conversations reopen, requiring context to be repeated, constraints to be re-explained, and priorities to be restated because the decision did not travel intact across the boundaries it crossed.

The following week leadership stays closer to the work. They respond faster to messages, offer clarification before it is requested, and join meetings they never used to attend. Things begin to move again, but now they only move when leadership presence is applied. When presence recedes, questions pile up and momentum slows. The organization has not resisted the decision. It simply could not carry it on its own.

Nothing here looks like a breakdown. The teams are capable, the tools work, and the relationships are good. From the outside this looks like a healthy organization doing complex work. From the inside something feels heavier than it should. The strain is difficult to name but easy to feel. The work now requires translation at every step, and the system needs help to remember what it was told.

Governance did not fail; the decision was made clearly and communicated. Operations did not fail; the teams executed as best they could with what they had. What failed were the crossings between governance and execution. For the decision to move from the meeting room into action, it had to flow down through the Risk Stack™. It moved from governance into operations, but operations required data to flow to the right people at the right time. Data required integration so systems could share information cleanly. Integration required infrastructure to actually support the connections being asked of it. And all of that required identity so people had access to what they needed to do their jobs.

The decision moved down through the stack, and at every crossing something was lost. Context thinned as it moved from governance to operations. Ownership blurred as it crossed from operations to data. Meaning dissolved as it traveled through integration and infrastructure. By the time the decision reached the people who needed to act on it, the shape had changed so much that no one was sure what had actually been decided anymore.

This is where problems actually live. Not inside the layers where they can be assigned to a role or escalated to a leader, but in the spaces between layers where work crosses boundaries the organization was never designed to support. The decision left governance intact, but it could not survive the journey down through the stack because the spaces it crossed were never built to carry that much meaning without someone manually translating it at every step along the way.

And when the decision broke, the problem did not stay where it failed. It surfaced back up. Teams escalated. Questions multiplied. Leadership stepped in to clarify, reconnect, and retranslate what had been lost in motion. The problem traveled back up the Risk Stack™ until it reached someone who could carry the weight.

Once you see this, many familiar patterns start to make sense. The constant need to clarify things that should already be clear. The way certain decisions never quite hold once they move. The sense that progress depends less on design and more on staying close. None of that is random. It is the system telling you that the spaces between layers are carrying more load

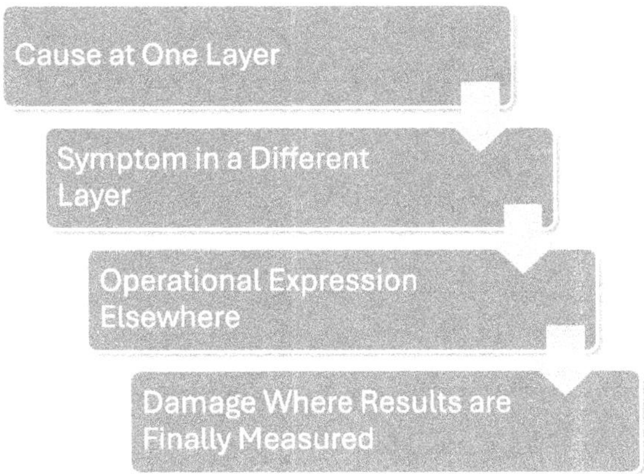

than they were ever designed to hold, and the only way that load is being carried is through people who step in to bridge what the structure cannot connect on its own.

But why have these spaces become so critical now? Because they were never designed to carry this much load.

Why the Spaces Became Load-Bearing

The spaces between layers were not always this critical. In simpler organizations, these crossings were shorter and more visible. The people involved shared context more easily, the systems were fewer, and dependencies were obvious. Work moved across boundaries, but those boundaries were thin enough that misalignment could be absorbed without much consequence. A handoff from one team to another might lose some nuance, but the gap was small enough that people could fill it informally without anyone noticing the structure had failed.

As organizations grew, the spaces expanded. More teams were added to handle complexity that one team could no longer manage alone. More systems were introduced to support work that had outgrown manual processes. More vendors were integrated to provide capacity the organization did not have internally. More platforms were adopted to connect everything together. Each addition made sense on its own and solved a real problem the organization was experiencing. But none of these additions were accompanied by a redesign of how work would move across the new boundaries being created.

The org chart stayed the same while the work moved differently. Roles stayed defined the way they were years ago while responsibility shifted to wherever the work actually landed. Systems stayed configured for processes that no longer reflected how decisions get made or how information flows. The structure remained static while everything it was designed to support continued to evolve, and the spaces between layers that used to be thin became dense with handoffs, integrations, external platforms, vendors, and informal workarounds that no one role fully owned and no single system was designed to support.

Today those spaces are not gaps anymore. They are the architecture. Work does not stay contained inside layers. It crosses constantly, and every crossing is a place where meaning can thin, where ownership can blur, and where context can dissolve. The more interconnected the organization becomes, the more these crossings multiply, and the more meaning must survive the journey between teams, tools, and decisions for work to hold its shape.

In practice, this shift rarely announces itself as structural. As complexity increases, handoffs require more clarification, informal tracking tools emerge, and leaders remain involved longer than intended. Nothing appears broken, and collaboration is often praised as maturity. Yet the work moves forward through coordination rather than structure, and effort quietly replaces design as the primary stabilizing force.

Without announcement or intent, the organization stops being structurally supported and becomes humanly supported. The architecture no longer carries the work on its own; people do. The spaces between functions, systems, teams, vendors, and decisions become the load-bearing structure of the business, even though they remain invisible in every formal representation of how the organization works. Org charts still show boxes, process maps still show steps, and accountability still appears contained, but none of those artifacts reflect where the effort is actually being applied.

This is why growth feels like strain instead of leverage, why scale amplifies fragility, and why leaders feel busier while results soften. Structure stopped compounding effort, and effort began compensating for structure. The spaces between layers are now carrying the organization, held together by judgment, memory, and vigilance rather than by design.

> When structure stops carrying weight, people start carrying it instead.

The Inversion

Once the spaces between layers become load-bearing, something fundamental inverts inside the organization. What began as temporary compensation for a structural gap becomes permanent infrastructure. What felt like responsible leadership stepping in to help work move becomes the operating model itself. The organization stops relying on its stated structure and starts relying on the lived one, and that lived structure is sustained by presence rather than design.

This inversion happens quietly and without announcement. No reorganization is declared, no new processes are formally introduced, and the org chart remains unchanged. Yet the architecture has already shifted beneath the surface. The system has learned where to go when it needs clarity, and it is no longer going where leaders think it is going. It is going where experience has taught it clarity actually lives.

Consider what happened to the decision we saw at the opening of this chapter. The decision was made clearly on Monday. By Friday it had split into versions as it moved through the organization. By the following week, leadership had to stay close just to keep it intact. That pattern did not stop after one decision. It repeated with the next decision and the one after that. Over time the organization learned that decisions do not hold on their own and that clarity resides with the leader who steps in to translate what the structure cannot preserve.

Soon every decision began to follow the same path. Teams checked before moving forward. Questions that once would have been resolved locally were escalated. People waited for leadership presence before acting on things that should have been clear from the start. Not because they lacked capability or confidence, but because experience had taught them that acting without confirmation often meant rework later. The cost of moving without checking became higher than the cost of waiting, so waiting became rational.

This is the moment the inversion becomes complete. Leadership presence is no longer support; it has become infrastructure. Momentum depends less on alignment and more on proximity to the people who can manually preserve meaning as work crosses boundaries.

The work itself is no longer the hardest part; keeping it coherent as it moves is. Execution is not where effort concentrates anymore. Preserving meaning across crossings is. The organization still produces results, but it does so by drawing down the energy and capacity of its people rather than being carried forward by its own structure.

The Cost of the Inversion

The cost shows up in your numbers. Leadership capacity becomes your constraint, margin compresses without explanation, and you lose competitive ground to organizations whose structure actually works.

Leadership capacity becomes finite in ways it was not before. Every hour spent manually bridging crossings is an hour not spent on strategy, direction, or building what comes next. Leadership time is limited, and once it is consumed by translation work that should be handled structurally, there is nothing left for the work only leadership can do. The organization cannot move faster than leadership can manually route work through the spaces between layers, which means growth is capped not by market opportunity or team capability but by how much weight leadership can personally carry.

Margin compresses without a clear explanation. Coordination overhead increases as more meetings are required to clarify what should already be clear. Rework multiplies as decisions that did not travel intact have to be corrected downstream. Cycle times stretch as work stalls at every crossing waiting for someone to manually reconnect what should have stayed connected. None of this shows up on your P&L as cost of broken structure, but it absolutely shows up in labor costs that rise faster than output, in delivery timelines that keep slipping, and in deals that take longer to close because internal friction bleeds through to customers.

When your competitors can move a decision from boardroom to execution in days because their layers are aligned and yours takes weeks because every crossing requires manual intervention, they outpace you. When they can scale without adding coordination overhead and you cannot scale without adding headcount just to bridge gaps, they operate at better margins. When their teams can act autonomously because the structure carries clarity and your teams have to check with leadership before moving, they execute faster. The gap widens not because they have better people or better strategy, but because their structure compounds effort while yours consumes it.

And here is what makes this so difficult to address. You are no longer fixing a surface problem; you are performing surgery on the architecture itself. Fixing where the problem shows up is a Band-Aid that stabilizes symptoms temporarily but leaves the source untouched. Fixing where the problem actually lives requires going to the crossings between layers where meaning is lost, ownership blurs, and context dissolves. It requires redesigning how work moves through those spaces so the structure can carry it without human translation at every step.

It is harder and slower, and it requires pausing to examine what has been avoided for years because it was easier to compensate than to fix. And in the short term it feels riskier than continuing to compensate because at least compensation keeps work moving even if it is exhausting everyone involved. But compensation has a ceiling. The organization can only grow as fast as leaders can manually bridge gaps, and those leaders will eventually hit a breaking point where they cannot sustain the load anymore. When that happens, the organization does not just slow down. It destabilizes because the invisible architecture those leaders were providing suddenly disappears and everything they were holding collapses at once.

This is structural debt. Every time you compensate instead of fix, you are borrowing against future capacity. Every crossing that requires manual intervention is weight that will need to be carried again and again until the structure is redesigned to carry it on its own. Just like financial debt, structural debt compounds. The longer it goes unaddressed, the more expensive it becomes to fix and the more it constrains what the organization can actually do.

> Compensation compounds until architecture collapses.

Once this becomes reliable, compensation becomes invisible. The organization no longer experiences this as drift or misalignment. It experiences this as "how things work around here." New employees learn the shortcuts immediately and are praised for figuring out how to navigate the complexity. Veterans become indispensable not because of their role but because of their tribal knowledge of which crossings break and who to go to when they do. The system organizes itself around people who can absorb ambiguity, and over time those people become load-bearing elements of the architecture without ever being named as such.

This is why attempts to fix the system later feel so difficult. Leaders are no longer working against misalignment alone. They are working against a new structure that has already formed, been socially reinforced, proven operationally efficient, and become emotionally defended. Removing it feels like removing stability even though it is the source of the strain. Continuity is chosen over change, compensation continues, and the architecture that is exhausting everyone gets hardened into place. This is not the moment when drift becomes a problem.

This is the moment when drift becomes self-protecting. The organization is no longer misaligned by accident. It is misaligned by adaptation. Until that inversion is seen, every attempt at improvement strengthens the wrong structure because it addresses what is visible on the surface while reinforcing what remains invisible beneath it.

What This Means for Leadership

By now something should feel different, not fixed or resolved, just clearer. The organization has not changed, but the way you are looking at it has. The strain that used to feel personal starts to feel structural. The friction that once felt like failure starts to feel located. What used to show up as constant pressure begins to take on a shape.

Most organizations do not break inside people, roles, or systems. They strain in the spaces between them. In the handoffs, in the transitions, in the places where meaning thins and ownership blurs and responsibility does not quite make it all the way through. Those spaces are easy to ignore because they do not belong to anyone, they do not show up on charts, and they do not fail loudly, yet they carry more load than almost anything else.

What is uncomfortable is how much of that compensation resembles what is usually called good leadership. Staying involved, being responsive, filling gaps before they turn into problems. Over time that becomes normal. The organization works, but it works because someone is always there holding it together. The cost builds quietly, not because anyone failed, but because the structure was never designed to carry this level of interdependence on its own.

Seeing this does not diminish leadership. It reframes what leadership actually is. It explains why so much effort has been required just to keep things moving. The issue was never that people were not capable or committed enough. The issue was that the work required a way of seeing that no one was taught. Often the real challenge was not managing complexity but understanding how complexity was already shaping outcomes through paths that were easy to miss.

At this point the organization starts to feel less mysterious even if it still feels demanding. The friction has a location. The exhaustion has an explanation. And that quiet thought that this should not be this hard stops feeling naive and starts to feel accurate.

What is still unresolved is something deeper. If breakdown forms in the spaces between, and if leaders have been compensating for architecture they could not see, then what does it mean when everything starts to feel chaotic, when outcomes feel unpredictable, when effort stops producing consistent results and you cannot quite trust the system to behave the way you expect?

This is where most conversations about complexity fall apart. Chaos gets treated as disorder, as randomness, as something to control or eliminate or just survive. But lived experience suggests something else. What feels chaotic is rarely unstructured. It is structured in ways that have drifted out of view.

Systems do not disappear when alignment is lost. Dependencies still exist. Incentives still shape behavior. Decisions still move. The order is still there. It just no longer matches the assumptions being used to make sense of what is happening. The structure keeps operating, but without alignment it becomes harder to recognize.

Once you allow for that, chaos starts to change its meaning. It stops being something to fear and starts becoming something to read. Not emotionally, but structurally. What feels unpredictable stops being noise and starts carrying information, a signal that something real is happening beneath the surface even if it is not obvious from where you are standing.

That shift matters. Because if chaos is not random, then it can be understood. And if it can be understood, you are no longer stuck reacting to surface-level disruption. You can start looking for the deeper order beneath it, even when that order has drifted far from alignment.

Chaos is not the absence of order. It is order that has drifted out of view.

And once you see that, unpredictability stops being a mystery and starts becoming a map. The spaces between layers are where that map is drawn. The crossings are where the signal lives. The breakdowns are where the structure is telling you it can no longer carry the load on its own.

What comes next is not about implementing the Risk Stack™. It is about examining that structure layer by layer so you can see where drift is forming and why it continues to surface in the same locations.

This is where the real work begins. The next seven chapters will take you through each layer of the Risk Stack™ so you can see where drift is forming in your organization.

CHAPTER 7

Identity Layer

This chapter introduces the first layer of the Risk Stack™. Before strain can travel between layers, it must begin somewhere. At the foundation of every organization sits identity, the layer that governs who can act, who can change things, and whose decisions carry consequence.

Defining Identity

An organization can feel fragile even when performance looks fine, and that fragility often begins in the structure through which authority actually operates.

This is rarely experienced as an identity problem. There is no department called identity and no dashboard tracking identity drift. Instead, it appears as friction. Decisions that should move cleanly stall without explanation. Routine work requires confirmation. Authority feels inconsistent even when roles are clearly defined. Hesitation and overreach appear in the wrong places, and uncertainty routes upward as the organization compensates for what it can no longer carry structurally. Nothing looks broken, yet nothing feels solid. This is the signature of identity drift.

Identity is often misunderstood because it is associated with culture, values, or behavior. In contained organizations that association was sufficient because intent traveled intact and context stayed close to action, making identity feel cultural rather than structural.

> Identity is structural. It determines who can act and whose actions carry consequence.

That assumption held only while work remained contained. Once execution spread across systems, vendors, automation, and distributed teams, identity stopped being a matter of belief and became a matter of authority. Culture cannot tell a system what it is allowed to do, and values cannot resolve conflicts between integrated platforms. Good intentions cannot substitute for clear decision rights once action is mediated by infrastructure. Identity becomes structural whether it is acknowledged or not. When it drifts, consequences rarely appear where access was granted. They appear later, often much later, where work breaks down or decisions lose force.

Most organizations assume identity is already settled. People have titles, systems have users, and vendors have credentials. Access exists because it was granted intentionally, usually under time pressure and in service of keeping work moving. From the outside this looks orderly. From the inside it feels manageable. Identity appears administrative rather than architectural. That assumption belongs to a world that no longer exists.

Modern organizations do not operate that way. Access is granted continuously without deliberate review. Systems are adopted to solve immediate problems, vendors are integrated to accelerate execution. Platforms connect persistently. Temporary permissions become permanent. Service accounts continue acting for people who no longer work at the company. Each access grant makes sense in isolation. Over time, those decisions accumulate into a structure of authority that no longer reflects current responsibility or intent.

This is where identity shifts from administrative to architectural, because identity governs who can act, not who should act. When those diverge, the organization does not break. It reroutes. Authority flows through paths no one explicitly designed. Every permission becomes a potential decision, and every credential becomes a vector of consequence. Identity drift rarely announces itself through failure; it appears as ambiguity. Responsibility feels shared while accountability thins, and exposure emerges without a clean line back to an originating decision.

When Identity Drifts

Identity drift rarely announces itself as a problem because nothing breaks when it begins. Systems continue operating, people continue performing, vendors deliver, and automations execute as scheduled. From the outside the organization looks intact. The shift is subtler than failure. Work still moves, but it moves differently. It feels heavier, less predictable, and more dependent on human attention than before.

Remember the example from the beginning of this book where someone left the company and still had access to email and internal systems six weeks later at a publicly traded firm. HR processed the termination paperwork, but the manager never triggered the access removal process. IT was never notified, and security had no issue to investigate. It was a complete failure, but it occurred in the space between them, where no one owned the process end to end.

This is identity drift in its purest form. Authority to grant access existed, and authority to remove access existed, but the connection between those two moments broke down because identity was never designed to carry consequence across the boundaries it needed to cross. HR owned termination. IT owned systems access. Security owned risk monitoring. Each fulfilled its responsibility within its domain, but no one owned the space where those domains were meant to connect. The person who left was no longer authorized to act, but the systems did not know that because identity could not travel from one layer to another without someone manually carrying it across.

> Identity drift rarely begins with failure; it begins when access and responsibility stop changing together.

One of the first places it becomes visible is in how decisions land. A decision is made with clarity, direction is given, and everyone leaves aligned in principle. But when its effects begin to surface, they do so unevenly. Some parts of the organization move immediately while others stall. Some systems reflect the change while others continue operating as if nothing happened. Ground that seemed settled must be revisited, not because of disagreement, but because the authority behind the decision fractures as it travels.

As identity drift deepens, leaders begin to notice changes without clear authorship. A workflow behaves differently. A configuration shifts. A system produces outcomes no one remembers approving. When the impact becomes visible, no one disputes that the action was allowed. The credentials were valid. The system functioned as configured. But when the decision is traced back to intent, the trail dissolves.

This creates a particular unease because consequence arrives without a moment of decision that anyone can point to. When authority no longer aligns with consequence, leadership becomes the place where the system reconciles the gap. When you spend more time clarifying who can act than actually acting, identity has already drifted. Over time the imbalance becomes structural. More actors gain the ability to influence outcomes while fewer remain clearly accountable. Vendors operate within contractual authority but remain outside organizational control. Automations execute decisions long after the assumptions that justified them have expired. Service accounts continue acting on behalf of roles that no longer exist.

This imbalance feels like weight because leaders are pulled into situations not because they failed to delegate, but because delegation no longer maps cleanly to consequence. Decisions escalate not because teams are incapable, but because authority is fragmented. Leaders sense that if they do not stay close, something will slip, and over time they normalize that instinct as leadership responsibility. Exceptions multiply quietly. Processes still work, but only after manual correction. "Just to be safe" becomes standard language, and approvals begin moving upward.

Another pattern emerges: dependence on specific individuals who become indispensable not because they hold formal authority, but because they understand where access truly resides. They know which permissions matter, which systems override others, and which automations silently execute decisions. They are not hoarding power; they are compensating for a system that no longer makes authority legible. Relief concentrates around those who can see the real authority paths, and anxiety rises when they are not involved.

As these conditions persist, the organization adapts around them. Leaders begin inserting themselves earlier to compensate for the fragmentation. None of this feels optional. It feels responsible. Yet it trains the organization to depend on leadership presence instead of structural clarity. The system continues to function, but only because someone absorbs the ambiguity. Over time, leaders stop expecting the organization to carry alignment on its own.

The Cost of Identity Drift

The cost appears in three areas: leadership capacity, accumulated risk, and competitive disadvantage. Leadership capacity is consumed by reconciliation work. Every hour spent clarifying who can approve a decision or reconcile conflicting authority, investigating how a change occurred without clear ownership, or resolving authority conflicts between systems is an hour not spent on strategy. Growth becomes constrained not by market opportunity, but by how much ambiguity leadership can personally absorb.

Risk accumulates quietly until consequence arrives. Access often persists long after responsibility shifts. Integrations continue operating under assumptions no one has revisited. Nothing appears broken until the moment impact becomes visible, and by then authority has already drifted from consequence.

You lose ground to competitors whose structure actually works. When their teams act autonomously because authority is clear and yours must check upward, they move faster. When their systems enforce boundaries and yours require manual oversight, they operate at lower cost. The gap widens not because they have better people, but because their identity layer aligns authority with consequence.

Identity drift does not arrive all at once. It builds quietly. Every permission granted without revisiting scope, every access path left in place after roles change, and every integration operating without defined boundaries adds weight the structure is no longer carrying. Nothing breaks immediately. The work simply requires more manual effort than it once did.

WHERE THIS SHOWS UP

Senior leadership should not be spending time on access rights, permissions, credentials, or deciding which vendors can modify which systems. That work lives elsewhere in the organization. And yet the consequences of those decisions keep landing on your desk, often months later and always at the moment when the cost is highest.

The same pattern appears when identity drift extends beyond internal systems and into vendor integrations. A regional services firm approves a new vendor platform to accelerate billing. The business case is sound, the contract is reviewed, and the integration launches on schedule. Invoices flow automatically. Revenue posts cleanly. For two weeks everything runs smoothly.

Then customer disputes spike. Finance freezes collections. Clients call confused about charges they do not recognize. The executive team is pulled into emergency meetings.

The root cause is straightforward. During implementation the vendor was granted direct access to modify billing logic without requiring internal review. The decision was intentional and made under time pressure to keep the project moving. The vendor was trusted, and the access made sense at launch.

What no one accounted for was what that access meant after go-live. The vendor continued operating within the permissions it had been given. Nothing malicious was occurring, and nothing was technically wrong. But no boundary had been designed between what the vendor could change and what required internal oversight. By the time the organization realized that boundary should have existed, downstream consequences were already visible to customers.

Now you are absorbing the impact of an access decision made months earlier by people several layers below you who were trying to move work forward. No single person failed. The system behaved as configured. But authority had drifted from consequence, and the gap only became visible once it reached the leadership layer.

The vendor relationship will be restructured. New controls will be introduced. The immediate issue will be contained. But the next instance will look different. A different vendor. A different system. A different access path granted under similar pressure. The pattern repeats because identity is still treated as administrative rather than architectural. What appears to be operational friction is structural misalignment moving upward through the stack.

This is the Risk Stack™ in motion. The problem began at identity when access was granted without defined boundaries. That permission, granted months earlier to accelerate execution, determined what could happen long before anyone felt the consequence. By the time leadership became aware, the decision had already cascaded through multiple layers. It surfaced as customer disputes and erosion of trust. The problem did not start where it showed up. It started when authority was granted without accounting for how it would operate once the system went live.

What the Risk Stack™ Reveals

Access rights, permissions, and system credentials are decisions normally made far from senior leadership, handled by teams responsible for identity administration and technical controls. They surface later, often months after the original decision, at the exact moment when risk, cost, or consequence becomes unavoidable.

In those moments nothing appears broken. The right people were in the room. The process was followed. The systems functioned as designed. Everyone acted within the access they were given. There is no clear failure to correct and no obvious rule that was violated. And yet the decision cannot resolve itself. It requires someone with enough standing to reconcile competing permissions, overlapping authority, or ownership that exists on paper but not in practice. That load lands at the leadership layer, where the system ultimately reconciles the misalignment.

What is happening underneath is structural. Identity, understood as who can act, has drifted from responsibility and intent. Access persists longer than relevance. Permissions accumulate faster than they are revisited. Vendors operate with authority that was never scoped for what they would do after go-live. None of this is malicious. It is simply what happens when organizations grow without revisiting how authority actually moves through the system.

The Risk Stack™ reveals that identity governs who has the right to make decisions that carry impact. When identity drifts, those decisions route upward until they find a place where consequence can be absorbed. That place is leadership, not because leaders are meant to own every decision, but because they are the only ones with enough authority to reconcile misalignment across systems, roles, and contracts that no longer align cleanly. This is what identity failure looks like: not collapse, but a steady transfer of structural load upward. Work continues to move and the organization appears healthy, but alignment has thinned and leadership is absorbing the cost.

> When authority no longer aligns with consequence,
> leadership becomes the place where the system reconciles
> the gap.

What Changes Once Identity Is Seen Clearly

Once you see identity clearly, the question shifts from "why is this on my desk again?" to "who was granted access to make this decision, and why does that authority no longer match reality?"

Remember the person who left the company but still had access six weeks later at a publicly traded firm. That was not just a process failure. It was regulatory exposure, a security breach, and liability that could have triggered an SEC inquiry, destroyed customer trust, or placed competitive intelligence in the wrong hands. It surfaced only because someone eventually noticed and escalated it. Before seeing identity as a layer, that incident gets treated as a one-off mistake. Someone is reminded to follow process, and the organization moves on. After seeing identity clearly, you recognize the pattern: access was granted, roles changed, and nothing connected those two moments structurally. The escalation is not the problem. It is the signal that authority and consequence have drifted apart.

You can distinguish between decisions that require your judgment and escalations that reveal identity gaps the structure should be closing on its own. You are not here to manage permissions. You are here to recognize when the organization is routing compensation into your capacity because authority no longer aligns with consequence.

The weight does not disappear, but it becomes manageable because you understand where it originates. Once you see identity clearly, you realize you have been solving the wrong problem and can finally stop carrying weight that does not belong to you.

CHAPTER 8

Infrastructure Layer

This chapter turns from who can act to what becomes possible once action begins. Identity determines who has the authority to act. Infrastructure determines what the organization can actually execute once the decision on how to act is made. When this layer aligns with how the business actually operates, decisions translate cleanly into action. When it drifts, effort increases while outcomes degrade. To understand why an organization feels slower, heavier, and more resistant to change than their strategy suggests, we must examine the layer that quietly governs possibility.

Defining Infrastructure

There is no dashboard tracking infrastructure drift, and no single leader is responsible for the environment through which all work moves. Systems have owners, vendors have contracts, and platforms have administrators, but the environment created by their interaction is rarely treated as a structural layer. Instead, the signals appear as friction. Changes that should move quickly stall inside platforms no one fully understands. Routine adjustments ripple into systems that were never meant to be affected. Capable people spend more time navigating tools than executing the strategy those tools were meant to support. Nothing looks broken, yet nothing moves easily. This is the signature of infrastructure drift.

Infrastructure is often misunderstood because it is associated with technology rather than structure. In contained organizations, that association was sufficient because systems primarily supported work rather than governed it. Platforms stored information, tools helped teams coordinate, and most decisions still moved directly through people. Infrastructure felt supportive rather than consequential.

> Infrastructure quietly determines what an organization can actually do, regardless of what its strategy intends.

That assumption held only while work remained relatively contained. Once execution spread across cloud platforms, vendor systems, APIs, automation, and distribution tools, infrastructure stopped being a support layer and became the environment decisions must travel through. Strategy can set direction, but infrastructure determines whether you can actually move in that direction. Platforms enforce sequences, integrations control how information flows, and vendor systems introduce rules that the organization does not fully control. Infrastructure quietly determines what is easy, what is slow, and what is nearly impossible regardless of intent.

Most organizations assume infrastructure is already settled. Systems have been purchased, platforms have been implemented, and integrations have been built. Tools exist because they were adopted intentionally, usually under time pressure and in the name of keeping work moving. From the outside, the environment appears stable. From the inside, it feels manageable. Infrastructure appears operational rather than architectural. That assumption belongs to a world that no longer exists.

The challenge is that this environment is rarely designed as a whole. Modern organizations do not operate inside a single coordinated system. They operate inside environments assembled over time. Platforms update continuously without organizational coordination. Vendor tools introduce new capabilities and constraints through release cycles outside the company's control. Integrations persist long after their original context disappears. Configurations designed for earlier stages of the business remain embedded in systems that continue shaping present decisions. Each addition makes sense in isolation. Over time those additions accumulate into an environment that no longer reflects how the organization actually works.

This is where infrastructure shifts from operational to architectural. Infrastructure governs what becomes possible once someone is authorized to act. When the infrastructure environment drifts from the way the business actually operates, the organization does not stop functioning. It adapts. Work routes around systems that prevent execution. People compensate for integrations that distort decisions as they move across platforms. Effort increases to carry outcomes the infrastructure environment can no longer support cleanly.

When Infrastructure Drifts

Infrastructure drift rarely appears as a system failure. Systems go down all the time, and everyone knows how to respond. Tickets get opened, vendors get called, patches get applied, and service is restored. That kind of failure is loud, contained, and temporary. What gets missed is the failure that happens when systems stay up but stop carrying the business the way they once did. It hides inside everything working while outcomes quietly degrade.

This drift first becomes visible in decisions that should be straightforward but are not. A change is approved, the intent is clear, and the work begins but slows almost immediately. Not because people are resisting it but because the systems your organization depends on cannot absorb the change cleanly. A platform enforces a sequence that no longer matches how work is supposed to move. An external vendor becomes a gatekeeper for something that used to be handled internally. The concept around the change itself is sound, but the infrastructure cannot support it. Execution does not fail; it distorts.

The arrival of AI exposes this problem faster than most organizations expect. When you introduce AI into an environment like this, the distortion accelerates. What once took days to surface now surfaces in seconds. AI does not improve judgment or clarify intent; it removes time, which previously allowed for correction, clarification, and the informal coordination that kept imperfect systems functional. Most organizations operate successfully only because capable people constantly reconcile inconsistencies, bridge system gaps, and apply judgment where rules fall short. AI removes that buffer. When timeframes compress from days into seconds, those human compensations disappear and the organization is forced to operate as it actually is. Automated customer service bots reveal that ownership of customer outcomes was never clearly defined. Automated approval systems expose that criteria functioned more as guidelines than rules. The AI works perfectly, but the infrastructure underneath it does not.

Over time, people stop expecting work to flow through the process and start navigating around the systems instead. Success becomes less about doing the right thing and more about knowing which platform will resist, which integration will lag, and which workaround will keep things moving. This knowledge is rarely documented so it becomes tribal. Teams that know the terrain move faster than teams that do not, even when they are following the same process on paper. What shows up as inconsistency is infrastructure enforcing different rule sets across the same workflow.

> Infrastructure drift begins when systems that once supported the business begin shaping how the business must operate.

Hesitation follows naturally. Approvals pause around changes that once would have been routine, because the systems involved make outcomes harder to predict. A configuration change in one platform may alter the output somewhere else. A routine update may break an integration that no one actively owns. Over time, the organization learns where change carries hidden cost and hesitation becomes reflexive. This is learned behavior shaped by infrastructure that reacts unpredictably to movement.

When people hesitate before doing what they are authorized to do, infrastructure has already begun teaching them to fear the environment.

The most dangerous pattern emerges when consequences surface far from the moment of intent. A decision is approved, implemented, and forgotten only to reappear weeks or months later as a billing issue, a reporting discrepancy, a customer complaint, or an audit question. No one connects the outcome to the original decision because no one was actively watching the path that ran between systems. Infrastructure carried the decision forward faithfully but not transparently. Fallout lands at the leadership layer because the environment translated the decisions in ways no one fully understood at the time.

Because these failures surface as execution issues, the response almost always lands on the wrong layer. Direction gets clarified, behavior gets adjusted, and oversight increases. The infrastructure remains unquestioned because it is still operational. Systems are up, vendors are meeting SLAs, and nothing is technically broken. The drift continues because the design itself is never revisited.

Over time the organization stops adapting to the business and starts adapting to the systems. The CRM you spent millions on five years ago is now a boat anchor dragging the organization down, because it was configured for a business you no longer run. The problem is not the vendor. The problem is that you keep investing in tools built for the organization you used to be instead of redesigning the way the business operates for the organization you need to become.

The Cost of Infrastructure Drift

The cost appears in three places: execution speed, adaptability, and the illusion of progress. Execution speed degrades because the environment between decision and outcome is full of friction. Every decision that must be manually routed because systems cannot carry it forward loses momentum. Every change that requires coordination across platforms that were never designed to communicate adds days or weeks the work itself did not need. Initiatives are reshaped to fit what systems can absorb rather than what the business actually needs. You are slow because the infrastructure forces detours around constraints frozen into platforms years ago. The organization moves at the speed the infrastructure allows, not the speed the strategy requires.

Adaptability erodes because infrastructure drift quietly removes change as an option. When the infrastructure was designed for a business you no longer run, every pivot becomes a renovation project. You cannot launch a new pricing model because the billing system was configured for a different revenue structure. You cannot consolidate teams because their platforms enforce incompatible rules. You cannot respond to market shifts because the systems underneath must be rebuilt before they can support something new. Competitors whose infrastructure reflects how they operate today move forward while you are still determining whether the move is technically possible. You are losing ground because your environment cannot execute the strategy you already have.

The most deceptive cost of infrastructure drift is the illusion of progress. Budgets are approved, tools are added, dashboards are built, and transformation initiatives are launched. From the outside, this looks like forward motion. However, none of these additions address the fact that the infrastructure environment itself no longer reflects how the business actually operates. Workload complexity increases while the underlying constraints remain untouched. You are not investing in capability. You are investing in workarounds, and each workaround becomes permanent once someone builds a process around it.

Infrastructure drift does not arrive all at once. Systems that once supported the business remain in place long after the business has changed. Integrations designed as temporary solutions become permanent pathways. Platforms continue enforcing rules that reflect priorities from years earlier. Nothing fails immediately. The environment simply requires more effort than it once did to produce the same outcomes.

WHERE THIS SHOWS UP

You are not supposed to be debugging platform behavior. Senior leadership should not be investigating why customer inquiries route to the wrong teams or why system logic produces outcomes no one intended. That work lives elsewhere in the organization. And yet the consequences of those systems keep surfacing at the leadership layer, often long after an original decision was made and always at the moment when the cost is highest.

Let's say a mid-sized financial services company decides to deploy an AI-powered customer service bot to reduce response times and scale support without adding headcount. The business case is solid. Customer inquiries are growing faster than the team can handle, response times are slipping, and the cost of scaling support traditionally is unsustainable. The AI vendor is reputable, the technology is proven, and leadership is aligned. The bot goes live and performs exactly as designed.

Within two weeks, the organization is in crisis. Customers are getting accurate answers faster than ever before, but they are also getting routed to the wrong teams and handed off between departments that do not own the outcomes the bot promised. Support tickets that used to resolve issues in one interaction now require three or four interactions because the bot is exposing something no one realized was broken: ownership of customer outcomes was never clearly defined across the organization.

Sales owns the customer relationship until the deal closes. Onboarding owns the first 90 days after the deal closes. Support owns ongoing inquiries, but only for specific product lines. Billing owns payment issues, but not disputes. Operations owns fulfillment, but not timeline commitments. Each function operates within its own boundaries, and each team has always relied on informal coordination to resolve anything that crosses those boundaries. The AI does not have informal relationships. It has rules, and the rules it was given assume ownership exists where it does not.

The bot works perfectly. It routes inquiries based on keywords, account status, and issue type exactly as it was trained to do. The problem is that the routing logic was built on top of an organizational structure that never actually supported clean handoffs. What used to be managed through human judgment and informal escalation is now happening at machine speed, and the cracks that were always there are suddenly impossible to ignore.

Customer complaints spike. Support teams are receiving inquiries they were never designed to handle. Sales is being pulled into post-sale issues because the bot does not know where sales' responsibility ends. Onboarding is fielding questions about products they do not support. Billing is escalating disputes to operations, and operations is escalating back because no one owns the resolution.

Leadership steps in to stabilize the situation. Routing rules get rewritten. Exception processes get added. Teams are told to coordinate more closely. The AI vendor is brought back to adjust the logic. Work continues, and customers stop complaining as loudly. These fixes are all manual interventions layered on top of the AI, rather than corrections to the structure underneath it. The bot still works. The organization is just working harder to compensate for what the bot revealed.

This is the Risk Stack™ in motion. The AI did not create the problem; it revealed it. Ownership of customer outcomes was never clearly defined once work crossed departmental boundaries, which meant identity at the organization level was already fragmented. Infrastructure then carried that fragmentation forward through routing systems and departmental platforms that were never designed to preserve ownership as work moved between them. When the AI began executing those rules at machine speed, the organization could no longer rely on human coordination to compensate. What had been manageable friction suddenly became visible failure.

Six months later, the company considers removing the bot because keeping it operational requires more leadership effort than the efficiency it was supposed to create. The AI succeeded but the infrastructure underneath it did not.

The business case was never wrong, but the assumption underneath it was. The organization believed it could accelerate customer service without addressing the fact that ownership, routing, and accountability were already fragmented inside the infrastructure responsible for executing that work. The AI did not create that fragmentation. It just removed the time buffer that allowed humans to compensate for it. What worked at human speed collapsed at machine pace, and no amount of AI readiness could have prevented that. You cannot accelerate what is already broken.

What the Risk Stack™ Reveals

You are not supposed to be managing platform conflicts, investigating why routine changes break integrations, or stepping in every time a system behaves unpredictably. That is not where senior leadership should spend its time. You do not configure the CRM, maintain vendor relationships at the technical level, or decide which API calls should fire in which sequence. That work lives somewhere else in the organization, handled by people whose job it is to administer infrastructure. And yet here you are again, pulled into another situation where the systems did exactly what they were configured to do, yet the business outcome is still wrong.

The pattern becomes familiar. Decisions are made cleanly, but the systems translating those decisions behave unpredictably. Consequences surface weeks or months later in places no one expected, and leadership steps in to reconcile outcomes the infrastructure should have carried on its own. From the outside this looks like hands-on leadership. In practice it is the same structural loop repeating: intent is set, systems distort it, and leadership absorbs the gap. You are not leading the business through infrastructure anymore. You have become the infrastructure.

At some point, you realize that this is not temporary. This is not a complexity you will outgrow. This is the operating model now, and it will not change unless the environment underneath it changes.

Infrastructure has drifted from the way the business actually operates. Platforms preserve configurations built for earlier priorities, integrations persist long after their original purpose disappears, and vendor systems continue enforcing rules that no longer match how work needs to move.

The Risk Stack™ reveals that infrastructure governs what becomes possible once someone is authorized to act. When infrastructure drifts, those possibilities narrow even as effort increases. Decisions route upward because the systems people depend on cannot reconcile intent with execution. Work arrives at leadership because the environment will not carry it forward without manual intervention.

This is what infrastructure failure looks like.

Until you see this clearly, you will keep applying effort where the infrastructure fails without ever addressing why it keeps failing in the same places.

What Changes Once Infrastructure Is Seen Clearly

Once you see infrastructure clearly, you stop mistaking operational involvement for strategic leadership. The question shifts from "How do I keep this moving?" to "Why does this require me at all?" Effort that once felt like hands-on leadership begins to reveal itself as compensation for an environment that no longer works.

This shift matters because you stop normalizing the weight. The loop that once felt inevitable becomes visible as a structural issue. You can distinguish between decisions that genuinely require leadership judgment and escalations that expose infrastructure gaps that should be resolved without you. What once looked like the cost of complexity begins to reveal itself as systems that no longer align with how the business actually operates.

Recognition does not immediately realign the infrastructure, but it changes where effort is applied. You stop asking teams to work harder inside systems that cannot carry the work and begin questioning whether the environment itself should still exist in its current form. The burden begins to lift because you are no longer treating infrastructure failures as leadership responsibilities. Instead, you can see clearly where the structure has drifted and where the real work must occur.

> When infrastructure drifts, leadership effort replaces the structural work the environment should be doing on its own.

Once infrastructure is visible as a layer, the illusion breaks. The systems are not supporting business; the business has been supporting the systems.

CHAPTER 9

Integration Layer

This chapter turns from what is possible to what survives as work moves. Infrastructure determines what the organization can technically do. Integration determines whether decisions retain their shape as they travel across systems, teams, and workflows. When integration aligns with how work actually flows, intent travels intact and outcomes reflect decisions. When it drifts, decisions are executed but arrive misshapen. To understand why capable organizations repeatedly revisit choices they believed were settled, we must examine the layer that governs continuity.

Defining Integration

An organization can make clear decisions and still struggle to see those decisions hold as they move. Direction is set, tradeoffs are debated, and authority is aligned, yet weeks later, the outcome looks subtly different from what was agreed upon. No single person changed it and no system visibly failed, yet the result arrives reshaped. When this pattern repeats, the issue is integration.

In the Risk Stack™, integration is not simply connectivity between systems. It is not APIs, middleware, or data transfer alone. Integration is the structural mechanism that preserves meaning as work crosses boundaries. It determines whether decisions retain their shape as they pass between teams, platforms, vendors, and workflows, or whether meaning gradually thins as work moves from one domain to another.

> Integration determines whether intent survives the journey from decision to outcome.

Modern work rarely stays inside a single component. A decision may originate in one meeting, move through multiple systems, pass between teams operating with different contexts, and surface weeks later as an operational outcome. Each participant may act responsibly within their domain, and each system may function exactly as designed. Distortion rarely occurs in a single place. It accumulates.

Consider a pricing exception approved at the leadership level. Sales records the deal in the CRM, but the system is not configured to store exceptions as structured data. Operations receives what appears to be standard pricing because the exception exists only in notes. Billing generates an invoice based on system defaults, and finance later discovers a discrepancy that creates downstream revenue recognition exposure. No individual failed, and no system malfunctioned. The decision simply did not survive the journey intact.

This is why integration sits directly above infrastructure in the Risk Stack™. Infrastructure determines what is technically possible once someone is authorized to act. Integration determines what is preserved as that action moves across systems and teams. Infrastructure governs capability, and integration governs continuity. When infrastructure drifts, decisions struggle to execute at all. When integration drifts, decisions execute but arrive altered.

Integration can erode gradually. At each crossing, a portion of intent is reinterpreted or lost. What surfaces is friction that requires increasing coordination, initiatives that stall between groups, and issues that reappear escalated without a clear origin.

Until integration is recognized as a structural layer, leaders will continue clarifying decisions that were already made, translating intent between teams that should already be aligned, and personally preserving continuity that the system should carry on its own. The exhaustion that follows is the predictable consequence of operating without structural continuity.

When Integration Drifts

Integration drift rarely announces itself through visible system failure. The shift is subtler. Work begins to require more coordination than expected, outcomes arrive reshaped, and decisions that once felt complete reappear in need of clarification.

Consider a decision approved with clear intent and agreement. Sales captures it in one system, operations processes it through another, billing invoices it according to standard configuration, and finance reconciles the numbers weeks later. Each team operates correctly, and each system behaves as configured, yet the outcome still diverges from the decision. The decision did not break in a single location. It degraded gradually across the handoffs between systems and teams.

This is often the first signal of integration drift. Decisions that appeared settled return for clarification. Meetings are called to realign work that was aligned in principle but distorted in transit. Leaders find themselves reconnecting fragments of intent that should have remained intact.

As drift deepens, hesitation begins to appear around routine change. A minor configuration update ripples unexpectedly into reporting, billing, or customer service workflows. Movement begins to feel risky because the connections between systems do not reliably preserve intent. Momentum gives way to caution.

Escalations also begin arriving without a clear origin. Problems surface late, and no one can identify precisely where the distortion formed because it did not originate in one place. It accumulated gradually. Each participant acted appropriately within their scope. The misalignment formed in the seams.

> Integration drift happens when decisions cross boundaries faster than meaning can travel with them.

Over time, certain individuals become indispensable because they understand where meaning is most likely to be lost. They know which integrations reshape data, which handoffs require translation, and which automations override assumptions embedded elsewhere. Their value lies in preserving continuity manually where the structure does not. When they are absent, progress slows because integration's weak points are no longer widely visible.

The organization continues to function, yet confidence in outcomes gradually shifts from structure to presence. Leaders stay closer to initiatives to ensure intent survives the journey across boundaries. What once moved cleanly now requires oversight to remain coherent.

Integration drift becomes normalized through adaptation. Meetings multiply, checkpoints are added, and escalation paths expand to compensate for the loss of fidelity across systems. These adjustments appear responsible, yet they are accommodations for a structure that no longer preserves meaning on its own. The cost is measured in lost momentum, absorbed leadership capacity, and the gradual erosion of leverage.

The Cost of Integration Drift

The cost shows up in outcome fidelity, organizational visibility, and leadership bandwidth consumed.

Outcome fidelity degrades because decisions that were clear when they were made no longer arrive intact. A pricing exception approved in one meeting appears in billing as standard pricing because the exception did not survive the handoff from sales to operations to finance. A product commitment reaches the customer without the conditions attached to it because those conditions only existed in conversations rather than structured systems. A strategic priority becomes interpreted differently by each team it touches because its meaning thinned out at every boundary it crossed.

The cost is the accumulation of outcomes that appear close enough to the original decision to pass review, but far enough off to create consequences weeks or months later. By the time the discrepancy surfaces, revenue may have been recognized incorrectly, customer expectations may already be set, or operational commitments may have been made against a version of intent that no longer matches the original decision. These are not simple mistakes.

Organizational visibility disappears because no one can trace where a distortion formed. When leaders ask what happened, every team provides a defensible explanation. Sales delivered what was agreed. Operations processed what was received from sales. Billing invoiced according to the contract. Finance reconciled according to standard practice. Each explanation is correct in isolation, yet the result no longer reflects the original decision. The decision simply degraded as it moved across those handoffs.

When the path between decision and outcome becomes opaque, the organization loses its ability to learn from its own failures. You cannot correct what you cannot trace, and you cannot trace what degraded gradually across boundaries no one originally designed to protec

Leadership bandwidth becomes the final cost. When integration cannot preserve meaning on its own, leaders become the connective tissue that holds decisions together as they move. Extra meetings occur to ensure previously made decisions survive the next handoff. Clarifications are issued for matters that should have already been clear. Leaders walk decisions across boundaries personally because experience has taught them that intent does not survive the journey unattended.

The cost is that the organization cannot move coherently without its leaders' presence. Every hour spent bridging gaps between systems and teams is an hour unavailable for work that genuinely requires leadership judgment.

Integration drift rarely announces itself as failure, because every component continues to function. The cost hides in outcomes that arrive slightly wrong, in problems no one can trace to their source, and in leadership calendars filled with meetings that exist only to preserve meaning as work crosses boundaries the structure was never designed to protect.

WHERE THIS SHOWS UP

The meeting begins with the expectation that this should be straightforward. The decision was made weeks ago, the direction was approved, and the work was reported as complete. As the first person begins to explain what happened, the tone shifts. The language becomes careful. The timeline adjusts. Something has been finished, but it has not quite landed.

The explanation arrives quickly. A dependency surfaced late. A vendor interpreted the requirement differently than expected. A downstream system processed the input exactly as designed, just not as intended. No one reacts with surprise because this story has been told before. No one is wrong. That is the problem.

The decision still exists everywhere it was recorded: in the deck where it was approved, in the email confirming direction, in the ticket that initiated execution, and in the system that processed the request. It simply no longer exists where the work is actually happening.

Each team describes their work accurately. The originating group delivered exactly what was asked. The receiving team explains why it could not be used as expected. The vendor points to the scope and contract language. Platform logs confirm normal behavior. Every explanation is true in isolation, yet somewhere between approval and delivery, the shape of the decision changed.

This is the moment leadership enters the conversation to reconnect the decision to its original intent. Exceptions are introduced so work can continue. Progress resumes, but only because someone manually carries the decision's meaning across a gap the structure could not bridge on its own.

When the meeting ends, the feeling is familiar: relief that the work is moving again, and unease because no one believes this will be the last time. The organization does what it always does. A note is added to the process. Another checkpoint is introduced. The next meeting is scheduled earlier. Each adjustment appears responsible, yet the pattern repeats anyway.

This is the Risk Stack™ in motion. The problem did not start where it surfaced. It began when the decision was approved, and no one had designed the connections required to preserve its meaning as it moved. Identity determined who could act on the decision. Infrastructure determined what was technically possible with the decision. Integration determined what was preserved of the decision. The decision crossed from sales to operations to billing to the vendor platform, and at each crossing something was lost.

From the outside, the organization still appears capable. Inside, momentum increasingly depends on leadership escorting decisions across boundaries. Nothing is broken enough to stop, and nothing is stable enough to trust completely. Leaders remain involved because without their presence outcomes feel unpredictable.

What the Risk Stack™

Reveals You are not supposed to be reconstructing decisions that were already made. That is not where leadership should spend its time. And yet here you are again, in another meeting where a decision approved weeks earlier has arrived reshaped, and no one can explain where it changed.

In those moments, nothing appears broken. The systems are operational, the teams delivered their work, and the vendors met their obligations. Everyone involved acted within their authority and followed the processes that existed. There is no clear failure to correct because meaning was lost somewhere in motion, and the only place it can be recovered is with you.

What is happening underneath is structural. Integration, understood as the connections between systems and teams, has drifted. Handoffs were designed when work was simpler and the boundaries were clearer. Systems were connected when dependencies were fewer, and context was easier to preserve. As the business evolved, those connections were never redesigned to carry the increased load, and meaning weakens as decisions move through seams.

The Risk Stack™ reveals that integration governs whether decisions remain intact as they move across systems and teams. When integration drifts, those decisions arrive distorted even when every component functions correctly. Work routes upward not because the connections between them cannot preserve intent on their own. Leadership becomes the place where meaning is reconstructed after it fractures in motion.

> When integration fails to preserve meaning, leadership becomes the layer that restores it.

This is what integration failure looks like: a steady transfer of coherence work upward. Decisions still get made and work still moves, but meaning no longer travels intact without leadership present. The organization continues to function, but only by consuming leadership capacity to reconstruct what should have remained whole on its own.

What Changes Once Integration Is Seen Clearly

Once you see integration clearly, you stop treating every reconstructed decision as a one-off failure. The question shifts from "What went wrong this time?" to "Where are the connections consistently breaking?" Effort that once felt like operational involvement begins to reveal itself as structural compensation.

This shift matters because you stop normalizing the weight. What once felt like unavoidable friction becomes visible as integration failure rather than execution weakness. You begin to see the difference between decisions that genuinely require leadership judgment and decisions that return because their original intent did not survive the journey across teams and systems.

Recognition does not immediately repair those distortions. Decisions that return for clarification are no longer interpreted as execution problems. Instead, they become signals that the structure responsible for preserving continuity has eroded.

Integration fails because it lives in the spaces no one owns: between systems, between teams, and between decision and execution. Once you recognize those spaces as structural rather than incidental, the problem changes shape. The issue is no longer what arrived broken. It is what happened while the decision was moving.

CHAPTER 10

Data Layer

This chapter turns from what survives motion to what remains true as work moves. Integration determines whether decisions retain their shape as they travel across systems, teams, and workflows. Data determines whether the reality those decisions depend on remains shared across the organization. When this layer holds, information carries shared truth and decisions propagate cleanly because everyone operates from the same terrain. When it drifts, numbers remain technically correct, but their meaning fractures across the organization, leaving leaders to reconcile competing versions of reality. To understand why capable organizations increasingly debate numbers that once settled decisions, we must examine the layer that governs shared truth.

Defining Data

Organizations rarely fail because they lack information. They struggle because they no longer share a common understanding of what is true. Reports are produced, dashboards are populated, and metrics circulate throughout the business, yet decisions increasingly require interpretation before action can follow. When this pattern repeats, the issue is not volume of information. It is the integrity of shared reality.

Data determines whether an organization shares a single version of reality as decisions move.

Data is often treated as something that exists to inform decisions, and when systems are simple and definitions are contained, that belief holds. Reports are trusted, dashboards feel authoritative, metrics travel upward, and decisions move downward with a shared sense of terrain. Disagreement may occur around strategy or interpretation, but not around the underlying facts. In that environment, better data appears to produce better alignment.

That assumption weakens as complexity increases, because data multiplies across systems built at different times for different purposes. Revenue may exist in multiple platforms. Customers may be represented in different states across systems. Performance may be measured on multiple timelines. Each system captures a portion of reality accurately but incompletely. What appears as a single number on a dashboard often reflects layers of assumptions about timing, scope, inclusion, exclusion, and transformation. The number may be technically correct, but teams no longer interpret it the same way.

Data continues to circulate throughout the organization, but fewer people can clearly explain how it was formed, what definitions govern it, or where its reliability ends. Information remains available, but authority gradually erodes. Data can inform discussion, yet it no longer resolves it.

Consider a company tracking customer retention. Years earlier, the definition was straightforward: a customer who renewed a contract was retained. One number represented one meaning. As the business evolved, subscription models were introduced, partnerships created shared accounts, and revenue recognition rules required alternative classifications. Finance calculated retention for accounting purposes. Sales measured retention to evaluate performance. Customer success tracked engagement using a different logic altogether. Each definition was reasonable within its domain. Over time, however, a single question began producing multiple defensible answers. The number remained accurate wherever it appeared, but its meaning diverged across the organization.

This is what the data layer governs within the Risk Stack™. Data determines whether information can carry shared truth across the organization as work moves. If integration governs whether intent survives motion, data governs whether reality remains consistent as it is measured and reported.

The danger is not disagreement, because disagreement can sharpen strategy. The danger is silent divergence, where multiple internally consistent data sets exist without a shared framework for reconciliation. Until data is recognized as a structural layer, the organization will continue producing information that no longer carries a single shared truth.

When Data Drifts

It is Sunday night before a board meeting, and you are still reconciling numbers that should already match. Revenue is finalized, but the version in the finance deck does not quite align with the version sales has been reporting. Both are accurate, and both pull from legitimate sources. The difference is small but large enough to notice, and you know someone on the board will ask about it. You sit with two spreadsheets open, because no one ever agreed on what revenue actually means when a deal closes in one system, invoices in another, and recognizes in a third.

You text the CFO and she walks you through her logic and it holds. Nothing seems wrong. You check with the VP of Sales and his number is different, but his logic also holds. He measures bookings by commit date, not close date. Again, nothing seems wrong. You are not looking at errors. You are looking at two versions of truth that diverged so long ago that no one remembers when they stopped meaning the same thing.

> Data drift begins when the same number can be correct in multiple places but mean different things.

Now you have to choose. Not which number is correct, because both are, but which truth you are willing to stand behind in a room full of people who assume there is only one correct answer. You know that whichever version you present, someone in your own organization will have a different answer if a board member asks them directly.

This is not how you planned to spend the night before a board meeting. You should be rehearsing the narrative, pressure-testing the strategy, and preparing for hard questions about the future. Instead, you are doing archaeology on your own data, reconstructing how a single number became multiple numbers and deciding which one you are willing to defend. Data drift does not appear as bad numbers, but as numbers that no longer settle decisions.

The instinctive response is predictable: more data, more dashboards, more metrics, more slices, more views. In practice, volume amplifies the very thing it was meant to resolve. When multiple versions of reality coexist without a shared framework, interpretation replaces decision-making, and data becomes something to negotiate rather than something to stand on.

This is the quiet failure of the data layer. It does not announce itself as an error because the numbers are accurate, the systems function, and the reports arrive on time. And yet decisions feel reversible even after they are made. Confidence erodes without a clear cause. Work slows, gets double-checked, and requires closer leadership presence because the organization no longer shares a stable truth beneath its choices.

Data drift does not feel like a data problem. It feels like the organization is losing its ability to commit, and you are the one left holding the gap.

The Cost of Data Drift

The cost appears in three places: decision velocity, organizational alignment, and risk exposure.

Decision velocity degrades because the organization can no longer move from question to commitment without stopping to reconcile competing numbers. Meetings stall while teams trace metrics back to their sources. Decisions are revisited within days because a different report tells a different story. The damage is systemic. The cycle time from question to committed action stretches across the organization, creating real cost in missed market windows, delayed responses to competitive shifts, and opportunities that expire while leadership is still trying to establish what is true. You are slow because the data beneath decisions cannot hold weight long enough for execution to begin.

Organizational alignment fractures without anyone realizing it has fractured. When sales measures success by one definition, finance measures it by another, and operations optimizes against a third, the organization is working in three different directions simultaneously. Each team is acting rationally within the version of reality their systems provide, and each believes it is aligned with the others because no one has realized that their numbers no longer mean the same thing. The cost is confident execution toward incompatible outcomes. By the time the collision becomes visible, it has already consumed resources, affected customers, and produced results no single team can fully explain. Misalignment rarely appears in planning meetings. It appears in customer escalations, missed quarters, or board questions that no one in the room can answer the same way twice.

Risk exposure compounds quietly because decisions made on fractured data carry consequences that surface long after the moment of commitment. You approve headcount based on a forecast that shifts three times before the quarter closes. You set pricing based on margin data that reflects averages that are no longer representative of the deals you are actually closing. You report numbers to a board that someone else in your own organization would present differently. None of these are errors. The risk is not that you will make a bad decision. The risk is that you will make a reasonable decision on a foundation that has shifted.

Data drift is not a problem you can solve with better dashboards. It is a structural failure in how truth travels through the organization. As long as that structure remains misaligned, decisions slow, alignment becomes harder to verify, and risk accumulates in places no one is actively monitoring. The organization does not become worse at making decisions. It becomes worse at knowing whether the decisions it has made are grounded in a shared reality.

WHERE THIS SHOWS UP

The meeting is full, and everyone is prepared. Slides are loaded, numbers are clean, and no one is bluffing. Revenue is up in one segment, flat in another, and down slightly in a third. Pipeline coverage looks healthy by one definition and thin by another. Churn appears stable overall but concentrated in accounts that do not fit the average. Every number on the screen is accurate, and that much is not in dispute, but what follows is hesitation.

Someone asks whether the trend is real or an artifact of how revenue is recorded across systems. Another points out that the number excludes renewals processed through a different platform. A third notes that the margin calculation assumes pricing rules that changed earlier in the year. Each explanation is technically correct, yet each produces a slightly different picture of the business. The conversation remains polite, thoughtful, and strangely unresolved because the data is doing its job technically, but not the job everyone hoped it would do. It is not settling anything. By the end of the meeting, no decision has been made because certainty never quite forms. The group agrees to revisit the issue next month, to keep an eye on it, and everyone leaves feeling uneasy. The numbers were solid, but no conclusion emerged.

This pattern repeats until it becomes the norm across the organization. Forecast reviews produce multiple projections depending on which assumptions drive the model. Pricing discussions stall because margin data reflects averages that no longer match current deals. Operational metrics appear stable only because variance has been smoothed out by aggregation. Each time the data is defensible, and each time leadership judgment resolves the gap.

Over time, meetings begin to change shape around this reality. Teams arrive with multiple views prepared in advance, knowing that one number will never be enough. Discussions stretch because nothing feels conclusive. Decisions get delayed, reframed, or softened. Leaders begin to be asked what the numbers really mean, and eventually the organization stops making decisions and starts scheduling decisions.

No one says the data is broken because the systems are working, reports are accurate, and dashboards are current. Nothing appears wrong, and yet leadership feels heavier than it should. Leaders make the call not because the data led them there but because someone has to decide.

This is the Risk Stack™ in motion. The problem did not start in this meeting. It began months or years earlier when definitions started to diverge, when systems aged without reconciliation, and when data multiplied faster than shared meaning could hold it together. By the time hesitation shows up in a leadership meeting, the drift has already traveled through the structure, and what leaders experience as a decision problem is actually a truth problem.

This is what data drift feels like in practice. The numbers that inform everything settle nothing.

What the Risk Stack™ Reveals

The Risk Stack™ reframes what leaders have been experiencing by showing that data drift is not a reporting problem, a technology problem, or an analytics problem. It is a structural problem that lives in how information moves across an organization that was never designed to preserve shared meaning at scale.

When work was vertical and contained, data moved short distances. A number was created, used, and retired within the same team or system. Meaning remained intact because context stayed close to the moment of use. Modern organizations do not operate that way. Data now moves laterally across teams, tools, vendors, and boundaries built at different times for different purposes. Every crossing becomes an opportunity for the data's meaning to weaken, shift, or fragment entirely. By the time a number reaches a leadership meeting, it may have passed through so many translations that no one can fully reconstruct what it meant at the source.

More metrics simply multiply the interpretations when the structure cannot preserve coherence. Leaders are overwhelmed because there is no shared truth underneath the information, and they must reconcile competing interpretations in every room they enter.

You may think the problem is that your data cannot settle arguments. The Risk Stack™ shows that this is the wrong question. The real question is when the organization lost its ability to share truth. Once you see that shift, dashboards stop looking like the solution and start looking like symptoms of a deeper structural fracture.

What leaders have been compensating for all along becomes visible. Data was never meant to persuade across boundaries; it was meant to coordinate across them. When that coordination fails, leadership becomes the coordinating layer by default. Conflicting versions of reality arrive in the same room, and someone must reconcile them.

> When data can no longer settle questions, leadership becomes the place where truth is reconstructed.

What Changes Once Data Is Seen

Clearly Seeing this does not reconcile definitions, align systems, or restore shared truth overnight. It changes where you look for the problem. You stop blaming dashboards, stop demanding more metrics, and stop wondering why capable people cannot agree on basic facts. Instead, you begin to see the structure that stopped preserving truth as information moved through the organization. Once that structure becomes visible, you know where the real work must occur.

Once the data layer is seen clearly, symptoms stop being misread as causes, and leaders begin trusting their experience again. The persistent sense that decisions should be easier than they are becomes a structural signal pointing toward something that can be addressed. The difficulty was real, and it now has a visible origin.

What changes first is not the quality of the data but the way leaders relate to it. Dashboards stop being treated as the final authority, and the expectation that clarity will eventually emerge from another report begins to fade. Instead of asking why decisions remain difficult, leaders begin asking where truth lost consistency. That shift moves the burden of sense-making out of individual meetings and back into the architecture of how information moves through the organization. The conversation in the room no longer feels like the problem; it becomes evidence of a deeper structural misalignment.

Preparation begins to feel different as well. Leaders still review the numbers before board meetings and still think carefully about how performance will be presented. When two versions of a metric fail to reconcile, however, instead of feeling like something should have been caught earlier, the discrepancy is recognized as evidence of definitions that diverged, systems that aged without alignment, and meaning that thinned as information moved across boundaries. The problem remains present, but it no longer rests entirely on the shoulders of the person trying to explain it.

This recognition restores proportion. Leaders stop forcing decisions prematurely to escape uncertainty and stop postponing decisions while waiting for numbers that will never fully agree. Disagreement no longer automatically signals conflict, and hesitation is no longer assumed to be weakness. Both can instead indicate that information has been asked to carry meaning farther than the structure supporting it can reliably hold. Seeing this difference reduces pressure without lowering standards. Decisions become more deliberate rather than slower, and conversations become shorter because leaders understand which questions data can answer and which ones it cannot.

Trust begins to change shape as well. Previously, leaders trusted data on principle while relying on judgment in practice, often feeling uneasy about the gap between the two. Once the data layer is visible, judgment no longer feels like a compromise. Leaders understand when data provides a solid foundation and when it cannot fully resolve the question being asked. The need to perform certainty disappears, replaced by a clearer understanding of where rigor ends and responsibility begins.

Attention also shifts toward where meaningful change must occur. The problem is traced back to the moment when definitions first diverged, when systems evolved without reconciliation, or when data began moving through boundaries that no longer preserved shared meaning. Leaders stop asking their teams to fix the reports and begin asking deeper questions about how truth travels through the organization.

Even with this clarity, however, something still feels unresolved. Shared truth makes decisions easier, but execution can still feel heavier than expected. Alignment may exist in the room, and the numbers may finally settle the argument, yet the work itself continues to struggle as it moves into action. Outcomes arrive later than anticipated or emerge in forms slightly different from what was agreed.

The friction at that point is no longer about truth but about movement. Data clarifies what is real, but it cannot carry that reality all the way to outcome on its own. That responsibility belongs to the next layer.

CHAPTER 11

Operations Layer

This chapter turns from what remains true to what actually moves. Data determines whether the organization shares a stable understanding of reality. Operations determines whether that shared reality can translate into sustained movement. When this layer holds, execution compounds and outcomes follow intent with little friction. When it drifts, work still moves, but it requires interpretation, negotiation, and constant human compensation. To understand why capable organizations feel productive yet strangely heavy in execution, we must examine the layer where theoretical decisions meet reality.

Defining Operations

Operations governs whether work can move from decision to outcome. Organizations often assume that once a decision is made, execution simply follows. When work stalls, distorts, or produces unexpected outcomes, the explanation usually lands on performance or discipline. Yet many execution failures originate earlier in the system, and operations becomes the layer where unresolved questions finally demand resolution.

Operations is not the place where intention is created. It is the place where intention encounters constraint. In the Risk Stack™, operations governs whether work can move from decision to outcome without being reinterpreted. It determines whether commitments made upstream can translate into movement downstream without requiring constant clarification, negotiation, or compensation.

> Operations determines whether decisions can survive contact with reality and still become outcomes.

Consider a customer commitment made by sales late in the week. By the time operations reviews it, the timeline assumes capacity that does not exist, and the scope depends on a configuration that was never built. The people responsible for delivery were not part of the negotiation and do not have the authority to renegotiate the terms. They have a deadline, a gap between what was promised and what is possible, and the responsibility to close that gap without eroding trust. In this moment, operations is interpreting a decision whose intent did not fully survive the journey from negotiation to execution.

Within the Risk Stack™, the layers discussed in previous chapters determine the conditions that make execution possible. Identity determines who can act. Infrastructure determines what systems and environments exist. Integration determines whether intent survives movement across systems and teams. Data determines whether shared truth holds across the organization. Operations determines whether all of that can translate into sustained movement. When the layers above are aligned, operations feels steady because work flows cleanly and outcomes match expectations. When those layers drift, operations is where that ambiguity finally surfaces.

Leaders often inherit a simpler model of execution. Strategy is set elsewhere, direction is clarified elsewhere, and operations receives that direction and turns it into output. If something goes wrong, the assumption is that execution failed, a process was not followed, or a step was missed. The solution becomes tighter procedures, reduced variation, and less discretion so that the system can perform reliably. In this model, operations is neutral and mechanical. It performs rather than interprets.

That model holds in smaller organizations where intent remains close to execution. The same people who set priorities experience the consequences directly. Context travels informally, exceptions remain visible, and processes flex because the people using them helped design them. As organizations grow, however, the distance between decision and execution expands. Work arrives at operations carrying assumptions that were never reconciled, timing mismatches between teams with different incentives, and constraints embedded in systems that no longer reflect how the business actually operates.

Operations is not simply a factory floor. It is the layer where abstract decisions encounter concrete reality. Where commitments collide with systems, vendors, and frontline constraints. When this layer holds, execution compounds and momentum builds. When it drifts, leaders repeatedly step in to reconcile gaps that should have been resolved structurally.

The danger is not that operations contains friction, because all execution does. The danger is mistaking interpretive strain for performance weakness. Until operations is seen as a structural layer, leaders will continue attempting to fix execution problems that were formed upstream. The organization will keep tightening processes while the ambiguity embedded in incoming work continues to accumulate. Operations will quietly carry the consequences of decisions that were never fully reconciled upstream.

When Operations Drifts

Operations drift rarely announces itself as concrete failure. Instead, it appears as accommodation. Workflow is adjusted to handle an edge case that no longer fits the original design. A handoff is softened to reduce friction between two teams that repeatedly stall at the same point. A step is quietly skipped because the information it depends on no longer arrives on time. These adjustments feel responsible because the organization is responding to reality rather than resisting it. Work continues to move, and that movement is taken as proof that operations is functioning properly. What is actually happening is the system is being rewritten without being redesigned.

The process still exists on paper. The diagram remains clean and the documented workflow still travels neatly from left to right. Yet the real work no longer follows the documented workflow. It forks, bends, and detours around steps that no longer make sense. It pauses where clarity once existed and accelerates where caution once lived. Because these changes emerge unintentionally, no one owns them. Drift appears as variation that cannot be explained, only managed.

The same work begins to take different paths depending on who touches it, when it arrives, or how much pressure the organization is under that week. One case moves cleanly while another stalls without obvious reasons. Teams construct local sequences that make sense within their own corner of the organization: reordering steps to compensate for missing information, adding checks to protect themselves from downstream consequences, and inserting informal approvals to avoid being surprised later. Each adjustment solves a real problem in the moment, but none of them gets to the root of the problem.

This is where the weight of drift begins to surface. Work slows not because employees are navigating invisible complexity. Every handoff begins to require context that the process no longer provides. Every exception requires judgment that the system cannot support. The safest way to move work forward becomes informal conversations rather than formal execution. Operations remains productive, yet it grows chaotic as people substitute coordination for clarity.

One of the clearest signals of operational drift is how often work must be explained. Tasks that should be clear within a stable system increasingly require contextualization before they can begin. Instructions grow longer, emails expand, and meetings begin with extended background so everyone has the same assumptions. Operations gradually relies more on narrative than structure because people carry meaning that the system no longer holds.

> Operational drift begins when people must carry context the process no longer can.

A second signal appears when only certain individuals can reliably move work forward. These people know which steps matter, which ones are ceremonial, and where the process must be adjusted to keep work moving. Their knowledge reflects the operational context the system no longer preserves.

The organization rarely names this pattern as drift because nothing about it feels optional. Deadlines still matter, customers still expect delivery, and revenue still depends on throughput. Operations continues doing what it has always done: absorbing pressure so outcomes can continue. The danger is not that operations adapts. The danger is that these adaptations quietly become permanent without ever being reconciled back into the design of the system itself.

The Cost of Operations Drift

The cost of operational drift generally appears in three places: throughput capacity, talent dependency, and the organization's ability to scale.

Throughput capacity shrinks because the organization spends increasing effort navigating work rather than producing it. Every task that requires ten minutes of explanation before it can begin subtracts ten minutes from execution. Every handoff that triggers a Slack thread to clarify what the process no longer communicates becomes coordination disguised as productivity. Every workaround that adds three steps to compensate for a system that should handle the task in one step becomes effort spent maintaining the illusion that operations still functions as designed. The organization pays for the full capacity of its workforce but receives only a fraction of it because the system consumes effort before it produces anything. The gap between what the organization should be able to deliver and what it actually delivers is a throughput tax imposed by a system that requires human compensation at every turn.

Talent dependency becomes the most dangerous cost because it remains invisible until it becomes catastrophic. Operational drift concentrates knowledge into the people who have learned to navigate it, and those individuals become load-bearing structures within the organization. They are not indispensable simply because they are exceptionally skilled. They become indispensable because the system no longer functions without someone who understands where it breaks, what steps can be skipped, and how to move work through pathways that no longer match the documented process. Over time, these individuals carry the operational memory that the system itself no longer holds. When these people inevitably burn out, they take the only reliable map of how work actually moves with them. When they leave, the organization often seizes. Hiring replacements does not resolve the problem because what was lost was not a skill set, but institutional memory that should have been embedded in the system.

The organization's ability to scale begins to erode quietly while leadership is still planning for growth. Every new product, new market, new customer segment, and increase in volume must pass through a system that requires manual intervention to function at its current load. The workarounds that kept work moving at one scale rarely stretch to the next. Informal coordination that once bridged gaps between teams becomes unsustainable when the number of teams doubles. The individuals who carried context cannot carry twice as much of it. Growth fails because the operational system was never designed for the volume leadership is now asking it to absorb, and no amount of hiring or tooling will change that when the constraint lies in the structure of the system itself.

Operational drift accumulates across all three of these dimensions simultaneously. Every workaround that quietly became permanent, every person who became a pillar, and every task that requires explanation before it can be executed adds weight. The longer this condition goes unaddressed, the more throughput it consumes, the more dependent the organization becomes on individuals who should not be carrying that burden, and the more difficult it becomes to grow. The organization is operating at whatever capacity the accumulated drift allows, and that ceiling gradually lowers the longer the underlying system remains unchanged.

WHERE THIS SHOWS UP

The vendor was not the problem. That conclusion came easily, almost too easily, and that should have been the first signal. They were responsive, their contract was clear, and their team showed up prepared.

They had done this work before, delivered similar projects elsewhere, and came recommended by firms the leadership team trusted. Nothing about the relationship raised concern. After months of internal debate, this was supposed to simplify things: a clean handoff, a contained scope, someone else carrying the load. At first, that is exactly what happened.

The kickoff was smooth. Roles were outlined, timelines were agreed upon, and integration points were identified. Everyone left the meeting with quiet confidence that the work would move forward without much attention, that operations would absorb it the way it always had, and that leadership could step back.

What followed was not vendor failure. It was the organization discovering how much it had already been compensating for.

Questions began to surface. They were not objections or red flags; they were simple clarifications. The vendor asked for confirmation on a requirement that had already been approved, and the question itself was straightforward even though the answer was not. The answer depended on how another team interpreted a policy that had been updated recently, and that team was not in the meeting. Someone offered an answer anyway, not because they were certain but because the work needed to keep moving. The vendor proceeded. Nothing stalled, nothing escalated, and the system absorbed the uncertainty and moved forward.

A week later, a deliverable arrived that technically met the requirement but did not quite fit the workflow it was meant to support. It was not incorrect, but it did not land cleanly. A small adjustment was requested, and the vendor agreed immediately. That adjustment, however, required input from another internal group, which triggered a separate conversation about priorities. The discussion resolved politely but vaguely because no one wanted to slow the project. Work moved forward again.

This pattern repeated quietly and efficiently. Each step forward carried a small translation. The vendor adjusted output to match internal feedback, internal teams adjusted expectations to match what the vendor could deliver within scope, and operations began filling the gaps. Someone created a manual step to reconcile two systems that were never designed to communicate with each other. Someone else documented a workaround so the next handoff would proceed more smoothly. None of these changes felt dramatic, and none of them appeared reckless.

There was no moment that demanded escalation and no single error that could be corrected. The project remained technically on track, milestones were met, and status updates sounded reasonable. From a distance, it appeared well-managed. From the inside, it felt heavier than it should have.

Leadership noticed the weight before they could explain it. They began joining more meetings and asking more questions. Decisions settled faster when leadership was present. The vendor appreciated the clarity, internal teams felt supported, and momentum improved. When leadership stepped back, the friction returned.

By the time the project was delivered, it was declared a success. The outcome met expectations, the vendor was paid, and the systems functioned, mostly. Leadership moved on. The cost was never fully tallied because it never appeared in the budget. It showed up in how operations had changed. Manual steps that were meant to be temporary became permanent. Extra checks remained in place because no one trusted the process to hold without them. Communication rituals replaced structure. The organization adapted around these additions because it had to.

The next project followed the same path, only faster. The workarounds were already in place, expectations were already lowered, and leadership involvement was assumed earlier.

This is the Risk Stack™ in motion. Operations did not fail. It revealed where alignment above it had already weakened. It exposed where intent lost force as it moved, where decisions never fully settled before execution began, and where leadership presence substituted for structural clarity. The system did not collapse because operations absorbed the misalignment, and that absorption was the signal of the shift.

The vendor moved on. The organization adapted. Operations changed again, doing what it always does when the architecture above it fails to resolve itself. It kept the work moving, but at a cost no one named.

What the Risk Stack™ Reveals

The Risk Stack™ reveals that operations is rarely the source of failure. It is the surface where failure finally becomes visible.

Leaders often spend years trying to fix execution. Processes are tightened, people are replaced, and new tools are introduced in the hope that operations will stabilize. Yet the problems return in slightly different forms. Work still slows, exceptions still multiply, and leadership presence remains necessary to keep initiatives moving. The reason becomes clear once the structure is visible.

Long before work slows, loops, or requires intervention, the conditions that produce those problems have already formed upstream. Authority has blurred, priorities have conflicted, and constraints have shifted. By the time work reaches operations it is no longer the raw, original intent. It is intent that has already been translated, compromised, conditionalized, and reshaped by every layer it passed. Operations is not where complexity is created. It is where complexity finally becomes unavoidable.

Every layer described in the Risk Stack™ appears here. Access granted without clear ownership shows up as identity leaking into operations. Systems that require manual workarounds to function reflect infrastructure the organization has already outgrown. Teams that cannot hand work off without a meeting reveal integration that was never designed to carry meaning on its own. Numbers no one trusts enough to act on signal data that stopped carrying a shared truth. Problems that surface in operations are the accumulated scar tissue of every upstream layer that drifted.

This is why operational fixes often feel both necessary and unsatisfying. Over time, operations becomes dense with procedure because it has become the place where unresolved structure is stored. Each fix becomes another layer of interpretation that operations must carry. Each new rule adds another decision point that requires judgment. Exceptions multiply because the structure above operations never fully reconciled the assumptions it passed downstream.

When operations absorbs unresolved ambiguity, leadership begins carrying work the system should have resolved upstream.

The Risk Stack™ reframes operational pressure as diagnostic information. The more leadership presence that is required to keep work moving, the more the system is relying on effort rather than alignment. Leaders are exhausted because operations is revealing misalignment everywhere, and leadership has become the mechanism that prevents that misalignment from stopping the work.

> When operations absorbs unresolved ambiguity, leadership begins carrying work the system should have resolved upstream.

What Changes Once Operations Is Seen Clearly

Once this becomes visible, operations becomes the layer leaders learn to read. Where does work require explanation before it can begin? Where do handoffs depend on conversation rather than process? Where does output rely on specific individuals being present? Where do exceptions begin to outnumber the normal path? These are not operational questions. They are architectural ones, and they point upstream to where the real work of alignment must occur.

Once the operations layer is seen clearly, the pressure leaders have been feeling finally begins to make sense. What looked like inefficiency was not waste, what felt like slowness was not a lack of discipline, and what appeared as constant friction was not poor execution. Operations has been carrying weight that never belonged to it, quietly compensating for ambiguity that should have been resolved long before work ever reached this layer.

Past experiences begin to take on new meaning. The exhaustion was real, and the frustration was justified. The suspicion leaders quietly carried that execution should not require this much effort was correct. Now the reason it was so difficult becomes visible.

The first shift is not procedural but perceptual. Leaders stop asking why teams cannot follow the workflow and begin asking what the workflow has been forced to absorb. Processes appear complex because reality has expanded beyond the structure that was meant to contain it. Shadow processes stop looking like rebellion and start looking like evidence, marking the places where intent cannot survive the journey from decision to execution without assistance.

As this understanding deepens, leadership effort begins to change shape. Interventions become less reactive and more purposeful. Leaders begin observing where operational effort spikes unnaturally, where handoffs require repeated explanation, where work cannot move without conversation, and where people must negotiate meaning before they can execute.

These moments become signals pointing upstream to decisions that were never fully settled.

Over time, operations begins to lighten. Teams spend less time improvising around uncertainty and more time executing within clearer boundaries. Operations returns to its proper role, the place where intent can finally move cleanly.

Leadership itself begins to feel different. Leaders still make difficult decisions and still carry the weight of outcomes. What changes is the nature of the effort required to move the organization forward. Leaders are no longer forced to serve as the bridge the system never built, the process that was never designed, or the mechanism that absorbs structural ambiguity.

Once this drift becomes visible, another question emerges. If operations has been carrying unresolved ambiguity, then where should that ambiguity have been resolved? If work consistently arrives incomplete, conditional, or conflicted, who had the authority to settle those conflicts before execution began? These questions belong to governance.

CHAPTER 12

Governance Layer

This chapter turns from what actually moves to where decisions are permitted to settle. Operations determines whether work can translate into movement once execution begins. Governance determines where that movement concludes. When this layer holds, decisions collapse cleanly, and direction carries through the organization without repeated negotiation. When the governance layer drifts, decisions continue to circulate long after they were made, returning under new conditions, new reviews, and new forums that slowly reshape their meaning. To understand why capable organizations repeatedly revisit decisions they believed were already settled, we must examine the layer that determines where authority finally closes.

Defining Governance Organizations often assume that once a decision is made, it will eventually move forward. When progress slows or outcomes fail to materialize, the explanation usually lands on execution, alignment, or competing priorities, but long before a decision reaches execution, governance has already shaped where it can go, who must authorize it, and which tradeoffs are permitted. In the Risk Stack™, governance is the structural layer that determines where decisions are allowed to settle. It defines authority boundaries, approval thresholds, escalation paths, and the forums in which tradeoffs are resolved. Governance determines not only who can decide, but where within the organizational structure a decision is allowed to close.

> Governance determines where authority is actually allowed to close.

Consider a pricing adjustment approved months earlier. Market conditions justified the change, data supported it, and leadership aligned around the direction. As the proposal moved forward, it passed through finance, legal, and compliance. Each review introduced conditions, each condition triggered additional analysis, and each analysis required another stakeholder. No one rejected the decision outright, and no one opposed the intent. Yet the decision entered a sequence of approvals and reviews that gradually reshaped its timeline. Months later, the decision remained unresolved and was revisited with new qualifiers attached while the market continued to evolve.

Within the Risk Stack™, each layer governs a different dimension of how work becomes possible. Identity determines who can act. Infrastructure determines what is technically possible. Integration determines whether intent survives movement across systems and teams. Data determines whether shared truth holds across the organization. Operations determines whether work can translate into sustained movement. Governance determines where decisions are permitted to conclude.

In smaller organizations, governance often remains informal. Authority stays close to the work and decisions are resolved through conversations rather than layered approval paths. Trust substitutes for policy, and shared memory substitutes for documentation. As organizations expand, risk distributes across functions, systems, vendors, and timelines. Governance responds by formalizing authority, introducing review forums, and defining approval thresholds designed to protect the enterprise.

Each addition addresses a legitimate concern. Over time, however, governance can shift from supporting judgment to directing outcomes. Decisions no longer move directly from intent to execution but are routed through pathways that reshape their timing, scope, and conditions.

The danger is not that governance introduces structure, because structure is necessary for scale. The danger is mistaking circulation for diligence and delay for rigor. Until governance is recognized as a structural layer, leaders will continue trying to accelerate decisions that are constrained by systemic design. The organization will interpret repeated review as caution while overlooking the fact that authority has diffused across several teams with no one holding the final decision-making power. Weight accumulates at the top because leadership presence becomes the only reliable mechanism that forces decisions to close.

When Governance Drifts

When governance drifts, decisions lose their gravity. Nothing breaks cleanly, and there is rarely a moment when a failure can be clearly named. Outcomes begin to feel underwhelming relative to the effort applied. Projects technically move forward but never quite arrive. Initiatives consume resources without producing the shift they were meant to create. Everyone agrees on the direction of travel, but momentum seems to dissolve somewhere between intent and execution. The organization appears busy, but very little that is decisive ever lands.

The earliest signal of governance drift is repetition. The same decisions return under slightly different names, the same risks are surfaced, acknowledged, and deferred, and the same priorities are reaffirmed before quietly being overridden by older priorities. Discussions begin to circle back on themselves because the organization struggles to hold the decisions it has already made.

This pattern often reveals itself in meetings that feel strangely familiar. The decision being discussed today was already approved months earlier, and you remember the tradeoffs, the alignment, and the agreement that was reached. Yet the same question has resurfaced as though it were new, requiring the same explanation and negotiation all over again. No one is being deliberately difficult, and no one appears to be resisting the direction. The organization simply could not hold the decision once it was made, so the entire discussion must occur again.

From the inside, governance drift feels like erosion. Leaders push and the system yields slightly, but nothing actually moves forward. The organization is not fighting the intervention, but it is absorbing it, metabolizing each effort into the existing structure without allowing that structure to change.

As this pattern continues, governance begins to reveal itself through contradiction. Speed may be declared a priority while approval layers multiply. Accountability is emphasized while authority becomes fragmented across committees and review groups. Innovation is encouraged, but exceptions are required for anything that deviates from established standards. None of these tensions appear unreasonable, because each rule and review process was created to protect something legitimate. The drift emerges in the way these mechanisms interact with one another. Governance stops resolving tradeoffs and begins preserving them.

Decision weight begins to concentrate higher in the organization. Matters that once would have settled close to the work begin to require senior presence. Meetings that previously resolved issues within teams now stall until an executive is present. What once flowed naturally through structure increasingly routes through individuals.

At first this shift can be confusing for leaders. The team appears capable, and on paper they possess both the authority and the information needed to make concrete decisions, but these decisions continue to return upward. Leaders often respond by encouraging greater ownership, reminding their teams that they have the authority to proceed. The teams acknowledge the message, but the decisions keep coming back.

Over time, it is clear the team has learned that decisions made without senior presence often fail to hold. Without visible authority in the room, closure tends to unravel later through additional reviews, secondary approvals, or competing interpretations of the original agreement. Teams wait for senior presence because they understand that decisions made in its absence rarely survive.

> Governance drift begins when decisions require authority to remain present in order to hold.

In this environment, the organization continues to function, but only because leaders become the mechanism that substitutes for resolution. Decisions close when they personally intervene, momentum resumes when they personally arbitrate tradeoffs, and alignment holds only as long as their presence remains visible. This produces a distinct form of exhaustion for leaders, not from the volume of work but from repeatedly revisiting decisions that were believed to be settled. The same conversations return months later under slightly different names, requiring the same tradeoffs to be weighed again. The structure that governance was meant to provide gradually gives way to a system that relies on individual authority.

The Cost of Governance Drift

The hidden cost is not abstract. It lands in strategic timing, leadership credibility, and organizational energy.

Strategic timing degrades because governance drift delays good decisions until they no longer matter. The pricing change you approved eight months ago was the best option when you approved it, but the market has since moved past the window where it would have made a difference. The product pivot that circulated through legal, compliance, and finance shipped late enough for a competitor to arrive first. The partnership everyone agreed made sense expired while terms were still being negotiated. All of these outcomes reflect a system that could preserve the value of the decisions moving through it. You are not making bad calls.

Leadership credibility erodes from the inside out. When a CEO sets direction and nothing changes, people notice. When alignment is declared in a room and dissolves within weeks, teams learn that decisions are not settlements but negotiations that never truly end. Over time, leadership direction stops being treated as something to execute and starts being treated as something to wait out. Board members begin to recognize the same initiatives reappearing under new names and start asking harder questions about what actually changes between cycles. Direct reports bring less of their best thinking forward because they have watched too many good ideas enter the governance system and never return. The damage is that people stop believing leadership decisions will hold. Once that belief erodes, it takes far more than a good decision to restore it.

Organizational energy drains in a way that does not show up on any dashboard. When capable people watch their work get absorbed without effect, they stop investing discretionary effort. The shift is rarely dramatic and almost never visible at first. It happens quietly. Some of the strongest contributors leave because they recognized that effort no longer produces outcomes. Others remain, but gradually do less, care less, and expect less. Organizations lose their vitality through a series of small withdrawals as people learn that the system will absorb whatever they give it without producing anything in return.

Governance drift widens over time. Every opportunity that closed while approvals circulated, every launch that shipped late, every contract that expired, every leader who left, and every hour spent re-deciding what had already been decided adds weight the organization must carry forward. You already feel the cost.

WHERE THIS SHOWS UP

You built this one yourself. The analysis, the business case, the strategy. You saw the market shift before anyone else and did the work to validate the opportunity. When you presented it to the leadership team, the response was everything you hoped for. No objections, no concerns, and a green light to proceed.

That was eleven months ago.

What happened next was not resistance. It was the Risk Stack™ in motion, each layer extracting its cost as your initiative tried to move.

The first friction came from identity. The initiative crossed business units, and no one could clarify who actually owned the decision to allocate resources. Three leaders had authority on paper, but none of them had authority in practice. You spent six weeks in conversations that felt productive but never led anywhere.

Then infrastructure surfaced. The systems required to execute the initiative had never been designed to work together. Data lived in three platforms that did not share definitions, and workarounds were possible but required manual effort no one had budgeted for. You adjusted the plan to accommodate the constraint, not realizing you were already beginning to shrink the outcome to fit the structure.

Integration came next. The initiative required handoffs between teams that had never worked together and did not share priorities. Context thinned at every boundary. Deliverables that were clear when they left one team arrived distorted at the next. You found yourself in meetings that existed only to re-explain what should have been understood, re-align teams that had already been aligned, and restate intent that had already been clear.

Data undermined confidence at every turn. The numbers that justified the initiative were calculated differently by finance, marketing, and operations. Each version was defensible, but none of them matched. You spent hours reconciling reports. By the time you arrived at a version everyone could accept, the original urgency had faded.

Operations revealed what the structure could not carry. The teams expected to execute the initiative were already stretched thin by workarounds from previous decisions. They supported the direction but could not absorb the work without dropping something else. No one wanted to name what would be dropped, so the conversation stalled.

Governance finished what the other layers had started. Budget reallocation triggered a review. The review triggered regional sign-off. Regional sign-off revealed unresolved questions from a previous initiative, and those questions required input from HR. HR needed alignment with the next fiscal cycle. Conditions accumulated while the scope narrowed and the timeline stretched. Each approval was granted, and each approval removed something from the original intent.

By month six, your initiative had a new name. By month eight, it had a new owner. By month eleven, it was technically still active but had been redefined so many times you no longer recognized it. The market opportunity it was designed to capture had narrowed, and the competitor it was meant to outmaneuver had already moved.

You sit in the quarterly review and watch your initiative listed as "in progress." Someone asks why it has taken so long, and the answer involves timelines, dependencies, and alignment challenges. You say nothing because there is nothing to say. The organizational structure worked exactly as designed. Every layer did its job, and the outcome is exactly what the structure was built to produce.

No one killed your initiative. It was processed layer by layer, from identity through governance, until what emerged bore no resemblance to what you proposed. You did everything right. The structure did everything right. And eleven months later, you have nothing to show for it but a line item that says, "In progress."

What the Risk Stack™ Reveals

The Risk Stack™ reveals that governance is not where decisions happen. It is where decisions are permitted to happen. By the time you enter the room, governance has already determined which decisions can close, who has the authority to close them, and how far those decisions can travel before they must be renegotiated.

You once believed the organization needed to move faster, commit more firmly, and stop relitigating what had already been agreed, but speed was never the issue. The structure had already determined what was allowed to move quickly and what was not. You were pushing against architecture rather than people.

This is why effort fails to produce lasting change. Leaders apply pressure, increase presence, and demand accountability. This sometimes works in the moment, because decisions do move when someone senior leans in. But the structure has not changed, and the next decision requires the same intervention, and the one after that. What looks like progress is actually override, and the system gradually learns that resolution only occurs through escalation. The pattern then reinforces itself.

Governance drift differs from drift in the other layers because it is self-concealing. It hides behind approval. It appears as diligence, risk management, and thoughtful oversight. Nothing appears broken because nothing is rejected outright. Decisions simply take longer, travel further, and arrive smaller than they began. The structure is functioning exactly as designed, which is precisely the problem.

The Risk Stack™ makes this visible by showing governance as a layer that can be read rather than merely experienced. Leaders begin to notice patterns. Where do decisions lose momentum? Where do approvals accumulate conditions? Where does authority fragment across roles that were never designed to share it? Where do tradeoffs remain preserved rather than resolved? These patterns are structural, and once they become visible, they stop being mistaken for culture, leadership style, or lack of commitment.

What the Risk Stack™ reveals most clearly is the relationship between governance and weight. Every decision that cannot be settled inside the structure must be settled outside it. Every tradeoff that governance preserves instead of resolving becomes a weight someone must carry. Leadership exhaustion is not a symptom of doing too much. It is a symptom of carrying what governance no longer holds.

Governance was never the obstacle. It was simply the architecture that determined where obstacles would appear. Once the architecture becomes visible, leaders stop fighting symptoms and begin seeing the design that produced them.

What Changes Once Governance Is Seen Clearly

Once governance becomes visible, the frustration that has been building for years finally has an explanation. The decisions that never landed, the initiatives that died by approval, the weight that kept concentrating upward, and the quiet sense that leadership should not be this hard all begin to make sense. None of it was random and none of it was inexplicable. It was a structure behaving exactly as a structure behaves.

The weight was real, and the exhaustion was real. You have been carrying it for years without being able to name it.

The first shift is relief, because the problem is finally located. You stop cycling through explanations that never quite fit. You stop wondering why decisions that should take a week take a quarter and whether your team lacks ownership. Governance was doing what governance was designed to do. The design simply no longer matched how decisions needed to move. That recognition alone changes the quality of the weight. It is still there, but it is no longer mysterious, and what is no longer mysterious can finally be addressed.

Once you see how governance shapes outcomes before decisions are even made, you become more careful about adding to the governance layer. Every new approval path, every new review cycle, and every new stakeholder requirement becomes weight the system will carry permanently. You begin asking different questions before adding processes. Will this help decisions settle, or will it add another layer they must survive? Will this clarify authority, or fragment it further? Will this resolve tradeoffs, or preserve them?

The third shift is diagnostic. You begin noticing where decisions slow, where authority fragments, and where tradeoffs are preserved instead of resolved. These patterns stop feeling like frustrations and start reading as information. You start recognizing which decisions close cleanly and which ones circulate, which forums produce resolution and which ones produce conditions. Your experience inside the organization becomes a source of insight rather than simply a source of exhaustion.

Leadership effort changes shape over time. Every decision that requires you to close it is evidence of where governance cannot hold on its own, and every meeting you attend because nothing moves without you becomes a marker of structural debt. Your calendar turns into a map of where the architecture needs attention. You are no longer guessing where the problems live.

Even when governance becomes clear, something remains unresolved. Decisions may settle cleanly, authority may hold, tradeoffs may collapse where they should, and the structure may function exactly as intended, but the organization still hesitates. Teams wait for confirmation before acting. Customers watch carefully to see whether commitments hold. Partners hedge their expectations. Employees move cautiously even when the path is clear. The mechanics are working, but something else is being evaluated beneath the surface.

> When governance cannot hold decisions in place, leadership becomes the structure that does.

What people are evaluating is not the decision itself but the pattern of decisions over time. They are watching to see whether this time will be different, whether what was agreed to will still be true when pressure arrives, whether authority will hold when tested, whether priorities will remain stable when the quarter becomes difficult, and whether the organization will follow through on what it said it would do. They have seen what happens when structure drifts, and they have absorbed the cost of decisions that did not land, commitments that did not hold, and priorities that shifted without warning. They are not resisting. They are protecting themselves from a pattern they have learned to expect.

This is where the Risk Stack™ leads. Through identity, infrastructure, integration, data, operations, and governance, each layer shapes the conditions under which work becomes possible. The final layer is not mechanical. It is not about systems, processes, or approval paths. It is about what accumulates when all the other layers hold over time. That accumulation is trust.

Trust is a layer that forms when the other layers stop contradicting each other. It grows slowly and erodes quickly. Trust is the evidence of alignment, not the cause of it.

CHAPTER 13

Trust Layer

This chapter turns from where decisions are permitted to settle to what remains once every other layer has done its work. Governance determines whether authority closes cleanly and tradeoffs resolve where they should. Trust determines whether those decisions, commitments, and outcomes are believed without constant reinforcement. It is the final layer of the Risk Stack™, formed through structural consistency repeated over time. When this layer holds, confidence compounds because work moves predictably and commitments survive without personal guarantees. When it drifts, the organization may continue functioning, but belief begins to thin, momentum weakens, and leadership presence becomes the substitute for reliability. To understand why capable organizations can still feel hollow, careful, and increasingly dependent on reassurance, we must examine the layer that registers whether the architecture beneath it can still carry belief.

Defining Trust

Organizations rarely collapse because of a single visible failure. More often, they slow down first. Clients request additional confirmation where they once moved forward quickly. Deals hover without objection yet fail to close. Forecasts remain technically sound while confidence in them quietly erodes. Nothing appears broken, and yet momentum weakens. When this pattern repeats, the issue is not reassurance or messaging. It is trust.

Trust is not sentiment, optimism, or personal rapport. In the Risk Stack™, trust is the structural verdict that forms after every other layer has already done its work. It reflects whether decisions travel cleanly, whether authority holds without reinforcement, whether commitments survive handoffs, and whether outcomes match expectations without constant oversight. Trust emerges when identity, infrastructure, integration, data, operations, and governance align consistently over time.

> Trust is the verdict the organization earns after every other layer has done its work.

When trust is strong, it is because alignment below is holding. Decisions settle where they should. Information carries shared meaning. Work moves without requiring constant clarification. Confidence forms not from explanation but from predictability. The organization earns belief by behaving consistently, and that belief compounds.

When trust weakens, the failure rarely originates at the trust layer itself. Ownership may have drifted. Infrastructure may no longer support how the business operates. Integration may distort intent as work moves. Data may produce multiple versions of truth. Operations may be absorbing ambiguity created upstream. Governance may prevent decisions from settling. Trust registers the accumulated effect of these misalignments. It is the final layer that signals the architecture beneath it is no longer carrying belief.

In smaller organizations, trust feels personal because structure and consequence remain close. Authority sits near the work, and promises are made and kept within contained systems. As organizations grow, decisions travel further and cross more boundaries. Authority fragments, work moves across incentives and timelines that do not align, and confidence becomes dependent on structure. When alignment weakens, leaders often compensate by increasing communication, presence, and reassurance. These interventions can stabilize confidence temporarily, but do not correct the architectural misalignment that produced the strain.

Trust does not disappear without cause. It weakens as decisions fail to settle, commitments require reinforcement, and predictability declines. The organization may continue functioning while belief gradually concentrates upward, resting on leadership presence rather than structural reliability. When trust eventually fails visibly, it appears sudden. In reality, it reflects structural erosion that has been accumulating over time.

The danger is mistaking visible reassurance for structural health. Until trust is understood as the final expression of architectural alignment, leaders will continue attempting to restore confidence through communication alone while the underlying layers remain unresolved. Confidence cannot be manufactured at the top of the stack. It is produced when the layers beneath it carry work consistently without contradiction.

When Trust Drifts

Trust drift announces itself as silence. The client who used to push back stops pushing back. You should feel relieved, but you are not, because pushback meant they were invested. The employee who used to argue for her ideas in meetings now nods and says, "Sounds good." She has stopped believing her input will change anything. The board member who once accepted your summary now asks for backup details. He is checking your work because he no longer trusts your word to carry it.

People do not fight systems they have stopped believing in. They simply stop bringing their full weight. They do what is required and protect what is theirs. The organization does not feel hostile. It feels hollow. Everyone is still present, still professional, still performing, but something that once flowed freely now has to be extracted.

> Trust drift begins when people start protecting themselves
> from the system instead of relying on it.

You start noticing who is cc'd on emails that used to be sent directly, how long it takes to receive responses that once arrived within hours, and the pause before people commit to anything. Hedge words creep into language that used to be direct. None of this is dramatic, and none of it triggers escalation, yet you feel the drag everywhere. Conversations take longer, decisions take longer, and everything slows because no one is leaning in anymore. They are leaning back, waiting to see what happens next before they expose themselves.

Deals that were ninety percent closed six weeks ago are still ninety percent closed. Renewals that once happened automatically now require executive involvement. The client does not say they are worried. They say they want to make sure everyone is aligned. They do not say they are evaluating alternatives. They say they are conducting due diligence. The language is professional, but the meaning is clear. They no longer believe your organization will deliver what it promises. They are not angry. They are careful, which means they have already started protecting themselves from you.

So, you step in. You get on the call personally. You give your word. You show up at the client site when you should be somewhere else, and you write the email that says, "I am personally committed to making this right." It works in the moment. The client stays, the deal closes, and the renewal gets signed. You begin making promises the system cannot keep without you standing behind them. Your calendar fills with maintaining relationships that once managed themselves, and your phone becomes the escalation path for issues that should never reach you. You are no longer leading. You are guaranteeing. Every guarantee you make teaches the system that it does not have to be trustworthy because you will cover the gap personally.

Inside the organization, the same pattern takes hold. You reassure the team that leadership is committed. You walk the floor more often so people can see that you are present. You send a note after the all-hands meeting that says your door is always open. You sit in meetings where your only role is to signal that the decision being discussed is real and will not be reversed next week. In those moments, you are not adding value. You are adding credibility that the structure can no longer supply on its own. Nothing moves without you.

When your best people stop fighting, trust has already drifted past the point of easy recovery. They fought because they believed it mattered. They stopped because they learned it did not. You will not receive an exit interview that says, "I lost trust in the system." You will hear something about an exciting opportunity, which is true, but the opportunity became exciting only after staying became pointless.

The cruelest part is that by the time you are working hard to maintain trust, the trust is already gone. The effort feels necessary because it is necessary, but it is not building anything. It is delaying collapse while the structure beneath continues to drift. You can feel the weight increasing and the margin shrinking, and you know, even if you cannot say it out loud, that this is not sustainable. You are holding something together that should be holding itself together, and eventually, your grip will not be enough.

The Cost of Trust Drift

The cost lands in three places that cannot be recovered once they are spent: revenue durability, institutional resilience, and personal lives.

Revenue durability deteriorates because trust erosion loses clients slowly through friction that makes every dollar harder to earn and keep. New business deals close slower because reputation precedes you, and prospects are watching how your existing clients behave before they commit. The pipeline looks healthy, but conversion rates are softening, sales cycles are stretching, and the cost of closing keeps rising. You are spending more energy to hold onto what you have while each new client produces less return, and the math is moving in a direction that effort alone cannot reverse. The clients who stay are simply staying because switching is expensive, and the moment that changes, they will leave without a conversation. You will not see it coming because they stopped telling you the truth months ago.

Institutional strength collapses because trust is what determines whether an organization can absorb a shock without breaking. When trust is intact, a bad quarter is a bad quarter. Leadership explains what happened, teams adjust, clients wait, and the organization moves forward. When trust has eroded, a bad quarter becomes a referendum on everything. The same event that a trusted organization absorbs and survives becomes the event that an untrusted organization does not recover from because there is no reserve of belief left to draw against. You have been spending that reserve for years to cover structural drift, and when you finally need it, the account is empty.

The personal cost is the one no one talks about because it does not belong on a dashboard. Trust erosion at this layer stops being organizational and becomes human. It is your health deteriorating because you have not slept well in months. It is your relationships weakening because you are never fully present anywhere except inside the crisis. It is your capacity to think clearly shrinking because every hour of every day is consumed by holding your business together. No other layer in this book demands this cost because no other layer concentrates this personally. Identity consumes leadership capacity, infrastructure consumes your calendar, data consumes decision confidence, operations consumes throughput, and governance consumes strategic momentum. Trust consumes you. Not your time or your attention or your energy, but you, the person underneath the title, the one who lies awake doing math at 3am, the one who smiles in meetings while calculating how long this can hold, the one whose entire life has contracted to make room for an organization that cannot stand on its own.

Trust drift collects payment in clients who leave without telling you why, board meetings that stop feeling like updates and start feeling like defenses, talent that walks out carrying everything the system refused to hold, partnerships that go quiet, teams that stop believing, and a life that keeps shrinking to make room for weight that was never yours to carry. You are paying for it in everything.

WHERE THIS SHOWS UP

The relationship had never required much attention, and that was part of what made it feel solid. Five years of steady revenue and mutual respect had produced conversations that were direct and commitments that meant something. You never tracked trust explicitly because there had never been a reason to. Work moved and outcomes followed. The relationship did not require maintenance because it simply held.

What you did not see was that trust had been quietly paying for problems the structure could not resolve.

The first signs were small enough to dismiss. A timeline slipped by two weeks, not a disaster, just a miss. You apologized, the client understood, and work continued. A month later, a deliverable arrived that technically met the requirements but missed the intent, and the client raised the issue politely and you fixed it quickly. No harm done. A quarter after that, there was confusion about the scope of a new phase and both sides remembered the conversation differently. You worked through it, found a compromise, and moved forward. Each moment had its own explanation, each explanation was reasonable. They felt like business.

But something was accumulating beneath the surface. Every slip, every miss, and every moment when the organization failed to deliver what was promised became a withdrawal from an account you did not realize had a balance. The client never said they were losing confidence. They simply began asking more questions, requesting documentation that once felt unnecessary, and cc'ing people who had previously been uninvolved. The tone remained professional, the relationship stayed cordial, and the distance grew so gradually that you mistook it for maturity.

Inside your organization, you were compensating without realizing it. You joined calls you did not need to because your presence reassured the client. You personally reviewed deliverables that should have been handled two levels down because you could not afford another miss. You sent the email after the meeting that said, "Just want to confirm we are aligned," because you had learned that alignment could no longer be assumed. You told yourself this was good account management. It was actually trust life support. You were manually supplying what the structure had stopped producing on its own.

The client saw it before you did. They saw that outcomes depended on your involvement, that when you were present things worked, and when you were not, things drifted. They interpreted this as structural weakness, because if the CEO has to be on every call to ensure delivery, what happens when the CEO is not available? They never asked that question out loud. They simply began planning for the answer.

The final moment was not dramatic. A commitment was missed that had been missed before, only slightly more visibly this time, and the client did not yell or threaten. They simply sent a short email requesting a call. On that call they thanked you for the partnership and informed you they would be transitioning to another provider. They had already made the decision, and this conversation was notification rather than negotiation. Five years of a relationship ended in a fifteen-minute call, and there was nothing you could say that would change it.

Walking out of that call, you replay the last two years in your mind looking for the moment it broke. You will not find it because there was no single moment. It was every structural failure that leadership absorbed instead of the system correcting it, every promise that required personal intervention to keep intact, and every withdrawal from the trust account that was never replenished by reliability.

Through the Risk Stack™ the failure becomes legible. Identity had drifted because authority and access were no longer structurally aligned, allowing commitments to change as work moved through the organization. Infrastructure had aged past the point where it could reliably support the commitments being made. Integration had fragmented as handoffs between teams lost fidelity and context disappeared at every boundary. Data had diverged until no one could confidently say if the client was receiving what had been promised. Operations had become dependent on workarounds and heroics to deliver what the structure could not reliably produce. Governance had hardened until decisions required escalation that delayed everything. Trust did not fail on its own. It was the final layer registering what had already failed beneath it.

The client did the math on whether your organization could deliver without you holding it together, and the math did not work in your favor. By the time you realized it, the decision had already been made. Trust was not lost in that final call. It had been spent slowly and invisibly until there was nothing left to withdraw.

What the Risk Stack™ Reveals

The Risk Stack™ reveals that trust was never something you could build directly. Every time you tried to restore confidence through effort, presence, or reassurance, you were treating a symptom while the cause continued to drift beneath you. Trust is not a lever to pull or a muscle to strengthen. It is the verdict the system delivers based on whether the layers beneath it are holding or failing. You cannot manufacture trust any more than you can manufacture a reputation. Both are earned by what the structure produces consistently over time, and both are destroyed when the structure stops delivering.

When the structure stops producing trust, leadership begins supplying it personally.

You have been trying to solve a trust problem, but you never had a trust problem. You had an architecture problem. This is the inversion the Risk Stack™ makes visible. Leaders exhaust themselves trying to rebuild confidence, and they blame themselves when it does not hold. They communicate more clearly, show up more often, make more personal commitments, and still watch trust weaken despite their best efforts.

Trust cannot be repaired at the trust layer because trust does not break at the trust layer. Repairing trust without repairing the structure is like repainting a wall while the foundation cracks beneath it.

The Risk Stack™ also explains why leadership presence works in the short term and fails in the long term. When you step in, trust temporarily returns because you are substituting for the structure. You are providing the clarity, the accountability, and the follow-through that the system cannot produce on its own. The client relaxes because you are personally guaranteeing the outcome, and the team moves because you are visibly committed. But the moment you step back, the same gaps reappear. You did not rebuild trust; you rented it.

What the Risk Stack™ reveals most clearly is why you are so tired. You have been carrying trust because the structure stopped carrying it. Every reassurance you offered was a weight the system should have held, every relationship you personally maintained was a connection the organization should have sustained, and every guarantee you made was a promise the architecture should have kept. You were not leading. You were load-bearing. The exhaustion you feel is evidence that too much has been displaced onto you because the layers beneath trust could not hold their share.

There is something that settles in this recognition. The weight was real and the exhaustion was earned, and it was never because you were not enough. It was because the structure asked you to be everything.

Once this is seen, the questions change. You stop asking how to rebuild trust and start asking where the structure failed to produce it. You stop chasing confidence and start examining what made confidence necessary in the first place. You trace backward through the layers. Where did authority stop holding? Where did infrastructure stop supporting the commitments being made? Where did handoffs lose fidelity? Where did data diverge from shared truth? Where did operations begin relying on heroics? Where did governance harden past the point where decisions could settle?

The Risk Stack™ does not offer a way to fix trust directly. It reveals where trust was never being produced. It shows where effort replaced structure and where leadership absorbed weight that did not belong to it. Trust becomes fragile when the layers beneath it fail to hold.

What Changes Once Trust Is Seen Clearly

Once trust is seen clearly, you are no longer debating whether something is wrong or trying to explain away what you have been feeling. The verdict the system has been delivering finally has a source, and that source is not you. The clients who pulled back, the partners who went quiet, the team that stopped carrying their full weight, and the exhaustion that would not lift were never the result of personal failure.

The weight was real, and now you know where it came from.

The first shift is interpretive. Trust is no longer treated as something to be managed, rebuilt, or reinforced through effort. It is understood as feedback. When confidence thins, you stop rushing to reassure and start paying attention to what trust is responding to. You look at whether authority is holding, whether decisions are landing, whether commitments are surviving handoffs, and whether the organization is behaving predictably enough to earn belief. The pressure to personally supply confidence gives way to a quieter clarity about what the system is producing.

The second shift is positional. You stop standing in the gap and start seeing the gap. Every place where your presence was required to restore momentum becomes visible as a marker of structural failure. You stop mistaking your exhaustion for dedication and start recognizing it as evidence that too much weight has concentrated at the top. Leadership becomes less about holding things together and more about understanding what should be holding on its own.

The third shift is relational. You stop carrying trust for the organization and begin allowing the organization to carry trust for itself. This is harder than it sounds, because the system has learned to depend on you, but continuing to substitute for structure only deepens this dependency. Trust does not rebuild because you show up more. It rebuilds when the layers beneath it resume their proper roles and begin producing without requiring your presence to guarantee it.

There is a version of leadership on the other side of this recognition that does not require you to be everywhere. Decisions settle without your involvement. Commitments hold without your guarantee. Clients trust the organization rather than only you. The structure carries what the structure should carry, and you are free to lead instead of compensate. Seeing the architecture does not reduce the weight. It restores proportion. What once felt like personal failure becomes structural signal. You stop fighting symptoms and start recognizing where the system itself is producing the outcome. The exhaustion remains, but it is no longer confusing.

You have now seen the full architecture: identity, infrastructure, integration, data, operations, governance, and trust. Seven layers that determine whether work can move, whether decisions can hold, whether commitments can survive, and whether belief can form. You have seen where the weight comes from and why it concentrates where it does. You have seen what you have been carrying and why it never became lighter no matter how hard you worked.

None of this makes leadership easier. It simply shows you where the weight has been hiding and how long you have been absorbing it. The patterns that once felt random now reveal themselves as structural, and structural problems do not resolve through effort. You cannot outwork misalignment. You cannot out-present a system that was never designed to carry itself.

What follows is not a framework for fixing this. The Risk Stack™ does not tell you what to do. It tells you what to see. The same meetings will occur, the same decisions will stall in familiar places, and the same initiatives will resurface under new names. The difference is that now you will understand why.

That is not relief. It is exposure. Exposure is where the real work begins.

CHAPTER 14

What Seeing Requires

Everything in the previous chapters explained how structural strain forms inside organizations. This chapter is different. It describes what happens when a leader finally sees that architecture clearly inside their own organization. Nothing about the environment changes immediately. The meetings are the same, the problems are the same, and the pressure is the same. What changes is how those experiences are understood.

The Shift

Nothing becomes easier once the system's architecture becomes visible. The work does not shrink and the stakes do not soften, but the source of the weight becomes clear. The friction that accumulated over the years was never random and it was never about you. It was structural.

The organization you were taught to lead was built for vertical authority, where decisions cascade down defined lines and work remains within stable boundaries. Work no longer moves that way. It now travels horizontally across teams, systems, vendors, partners, and approval paths that were never designed to coordinate with one another. The structure remained vertical while the work became horizontal, and that mismatch created weight with nowhere to go except upward.

For years the system kept moving because you kept catching what it dropped. When authority disappeared, priorities collided, or commitments began to drift, you stepped in so the work could continue. Because you caught it, the structural failure remained invisible. From the outside it looked like leadership. From the inside it felt like exhaustion.

At first nothing about your behavior changes. What changes is how you see. You sit in the same meetings you have attended many times before, listening to the same explanations for why something stalled or why the timeline must shift. In the past those moments felt like isolated obstacles that required intervention. Now they begin to look different.

You start noticing where authority disappears, where approval paths narrow intent, and where commitments weaken as they move through the organization. What once appeared to be disconnected problems begins to reveal a pattern. The same boundaries slow momentum, the same decisions struggle to close, and the same kinds of escalation keep returning to the same place.

Once that pattern becomes visible, the exhaustion begins to make sense. Your judgment reconciled conflicts that should never have existed, your credibility carried commitments across boundaries that could not sustain them, and your effort bridged gaps the architecture itself created. The same escalations may still appear and the same meetings may still dilute intent, but you now recognize the system producing those outcomes.

Seeing the architecture does not immediately change what you must do. The work is still there and the pressure has not disappeared. What changes is that the weight now has a visible source, and once you understand where that weight truly belongs, carrying it feels different.

The Leadership Trap

You did what you were trained to do. When things stalled, you stepped in. When decisions drifted, you clarified. When commitments began to slip, you reinforced them with your own credibility. And it worked. Meetings ended with alignment, projects moved forward again, and the client stayed.

Everyone moved on because you made it move. That is what capable leaders are expected to do.

The difficulty is that it kept happening. The stalls returned, the drift returned, and the same kinds of slippage appeared again under different names and in different quarters. Each time you intervened because intervention worked, and because it worked there was rarely a reason to question why it kept being necessary. The structure beneath you was failing quietly, and your competence was the reason no one had to notice.

This is the trap capable leaders fall into, and it resembles success from every angle. The organization gradually learns what you will carry and begins to rely on that pattern. Decisions that should settle elsewhere rise to you because resolving them yourself is faster than fixing why they floated upward in the first place. Conflicts between teams land on your desk because stepping in is easier than building the alignment that would prevent them from recurring. Trust that should be carried by the structure flows through you personally because you are reliable and the structure is not.

From the outside this appears to be strong leadership. You are present, engaged, and known as the person who makes things happen. From the inside it feels different. You rarely step away completely because you know what begins to slip when you are not there to catch it. Vacations feel risky, delegation feels uncertain, and your calendar fills with meetings that exist only because decisions cannot close without you in the room. Over time leadership begins to look less like direction and more like subsidy, as your presence quietly supplies what the structure itself cannot sustain.

Each intervention keeps work moving forward, but it also teaches the system something unintended. The organization learns that problems do not need to be resolved before they reach leadership because leadership will resolve them when they arrive. When priorities collide and you reconcile them, the system learns that priorities do not need to be reconciled earlier. When decisions drift upward and you close them, the system learns that decisions do not need to settle anywhere else. When trust thins and you steady it with your own credibility, the system learns that trust does not need to be embedded in how work moves through the organization.

> When structure cannot carry the work, leadership quietly becomes the system that holds it together.

Over time the consequences become visible. Decisions wait for you even when the people closest to the work understand them best. Clients trust you but hesitate with others on your team because confidence has been carried personally rather than structurally. New leaders struggle to gain traction regardless of their talent because ambiguity accumulated while you kept absorbing it instead of forcing it to settle.

None of this developed intentionally. It formed gradually around your willingness to carry whatever landed on you, and the organization slowly adjusted to that pattern. What began as leadership support became structural dependence. The organization did not drift because you failed. It drifted because you succeeded at carrying what the structure should have held, and that success allowed the architecture to weaken without anyone noticing.

Recognizing this pattern is uncomfortable because it means acknowledging something difficult: you have been solving the wrong problem with extraordinary skill. The organization did not need you to carry the system indefinitely. It needed a structure capable of carrying itself, and each time you stepped in you postponed the moment when that structure would have been forced to strengthen. The instincts that made you effective were the same instincts that allowed the architecture to weaken, and realizing that is not meant to be comfortable.

When the Architecture Holds

None of this means alignment is theoretical. It exists, and you have seen it before, even if you did not recognize what you were seeing at the time.

You walk into a board meeting prepared to present strategy instead of spending the first part of the meeting explaining why last quarter's numbers do not match what you projected. The numbers match because the commitments that were made held through execution. The teams responsible for delivery operated from the same assumptions the plan was built on, and nothing quietly shifted beneath the plan while leadership was focused elsewhere. You present what you came to present because the structure beneath the plan carried its share of the work.

A strategic initiative moves from planning to execution without becoming unrecognizable by the time it launches. The thing that ships is the thing that was approved. Scope does not quietly shrink because teams inherit constraints no one told them about, and timelines do not stretch because avoidable rework appears halfway through the process. What leadership approved is what the organization builds.

Budget season ends with decisions that hold. Resources are allocated, priorities are set, and months later those decisions are still intact. Teams are not quietly renegotiating what was already settled, and leaders are not reopening tradeoffs that should have been closed. The organization executes against what it agreed to rather than running a shadow process that undoes the outcomes of the official one.

These moments are not extraordinary. They are ordinary examples of what work feels like when leadership is not required to act as the connective tissue between every function and every decision.

Leadership still exists in that environment, but the work of leadership changes. Decisions still require judgment, tradeoffs still demand experience, and uncertainty does not disappear. What changes is where leadership energy goes. Leaders spend their time setting direction, making decisions that require institutional authority, and holding the organization accountable to what it said it would do. They are no longer bridging gaps the structure should close or translating between teams that should already share a common understanding.

Most leaders have experienced this at least briefly. There may have been a quarter when things moved without constant pressure from the top. A team operated cleanly without needing you to referee. A client relationship held because the delivery behind it was structurally sound rather than personally protected. Those moments rarely last when the surrounding architecture has drifted, but they are memorable precisely because the difference between leading and compensating becomes unmistakable.

That difference is what alignment produces. It does not create ease or perfection. It creates a structure that carries its own weight so leadership can finally focus on the work that only leadership can do.

Stewardship

You see the architecture now. You understand what you have been carrying, what it cost you, and what it cost the organization. You know what alignment looks like when the structure holds. The diagnosis is clear, yet most leaders who reach this point do not change anything.

They recognize the pattern and understand the cost intellectually. They can describe the trap they are in and still continue carrying the weight. This does not happen because they are weak or indifferent. It happens because everything around them reinforces the same pattern.

The organization has adapted to your presence. It has learned what you will carry and gradually stopped developing the capacity to carry those things itself. When you stop compensating, you are not returning the system to a neutral condition. You are removing a load-bearing element from a structure that has quietly been built around it. The system will strain. Things will slip. People who have never had to carry certain responsibilities will suddenly feel them, and many will question why you are allowing this strain to occur when you could resolve it yourself.

Your identity as a leader is also part of the trap. You became successful by being the person who steps in when things stall, who keeps work moving when others cannot, and who can be relied upon when everything else begins to fail. Over time this becomes more than a set of behaviors. It becomes part of how you understand your own value. Stepping back can feel like abandoning the very quality that made you effective, and the organization reinforces this constantly. Leaders are praised for being hands-on and rewarded for reliability. Almost no one rewards restraint or the decision to allow a system to struggle long enough to strengthen.

The tension between short-term cost and long-term benefit makes the decision even harder. When you stop catching something, the strain appears immediately and is highly visible. When the structure begins learning to carry its own weight, that learning happens slowly and is difficult to measure. Many leaders who attempt this encounter a moment when the first sign of struggle looks like evidence that they made a mistake, and the pressure to step back in becomes intense precisely because stepping in always works in the moment.

Beneath these pressures is something deeper than incentives or expectations. There is fear, and the fear is understandable. One fear is that the effort will fail. You endure the discomfort of stepping back, resist the urge to intervene, and watch the system strain. If the structure does not strengthen and instead collapses, it can feel as though you allowed the failure to happen for no reason.

Another fear is what the outcome might reveal. If you stop carrying the weight and the organization cannot stand on its own, that discovery forces difficult questions about what was built and how it survived for so long. Some leaders would rather continue carrying indefinitely than confront the possibility that the system cannot function without them.

There is also the fear of blame. If you step back and something fails visibly, the responsibility for that failure may fall on you. If you continue stepping in and exhausting yourself, no one can claim that you did not try. Carrying the weight can feel safer than allowing failure to appear in the open, and organizations often punish restraint more quickly than they punish burnout. These fears are not irrational. They reflect an accurate reading of systems that were never designed to reward the kind of restraint stewardship requires. A leader can work themselves to exhaustion without drawing criticism, yet a single visible failure can remain attached to them for years. Choosing a different path therefore requires more than insight. It requires the willingness to endure pressure from the very environment the leader is trying to improve. Stewardship requires choosing differently despite that pressure. It is the decision to allow the system to carry what it must eventually learn to carry itself. The organization may not recognize the value of restraint and the results may take time to appear, yet the alternative is permanent dependence. An organization that never has to support itself never learns how to do so, and a structure that is always subsidized never strengthens.

> Stewardship begins when leadership stops carrying what the system must learn to carry itself.

When the weight is never set down, it does not disappear. It is simply passed forward to the next leader, and then to the one after that, until someone finally forces the system to carry itself or the organization collapses under a dependency it can no longer sustain. The real question is not whether you are capable of carrying the weight, because you have already proven that. The question is whether you are willing to stop carrying it, knowing that the short-term cost will be visible and the long-term benefit uncertain.

That choice is rarely comfortable and rarely rewarded immediately. The structure may strain before it strengthens, and much of the environment around you will encourage you to step back in. Yet leaders who resist that pressure eventually discover something important: what first appears to be strong leadership can sometimes prevent the organization from becoming something that no longer needs to be carried.

Seeing Clearly

There is no resolution here. The Risk Stack™ does not tell you what to do. Its purpose is to show you what to see, and once you see it clearly the responsibility for what comes next cannot be handed back to the framework.

You have seen how the organization you were taught to lead no longer operates the way its structure assumes it does. Work shifted from vertical movement to horizontal coordination while the architecture remained largely unchanged. That mismatch created weight that had nowhere to go except upward. Over time that weight concentrated on leadership. Your competence concealed the structural strain, your effort delayed the moment when the system would have been forced to change, and your presence often became the substitute for an architecture that could no longer carry itself. You have also seen what alignment looks like when the structure holds and why many leaders who recognize this pattern still continue carrying the weight.

Tomorrow you will return to the same organization, the same meetings, and the same decisions that struggle to settle. The environment will look exactly as it did before, but the way you see it will be different. You will recognize the architecture operating beneath the surface, and when the familiar pull to step in appears you will understand more clearly what that intervention accomplishes and what it prevents.

This book was never meant to make leadership easier. Nothing could. What it can do is make leadership more honest by exposing the structure beneath the experience of leadership. Once the architecture becomes visible, it becomes difficult to pretend that effort alone will repair problems that only structure can resolve. It also becomes difficult to step in without recognizing the pattern that intervention sustains.

The architecture is visible now and what once lacked language now has a name. That recognition does not dictate action, advice, or methodology. It simply removes the ability to look away from what has been seen.

The book ends here, but the work does not.

Reading the Organization

After reading this book, the organization may begin to look different to you. Nothing about the structure itself has changed, but your ability to recognize it has. Moments that once felt like ordinary friction may now reveal something more specific underneath them.

This is not a method or a repair plan. It is simply a way of helping you read what you are now able to see. The patterns were always present. What has changed is your ability to recognize them more clearly.

What You Will Start to Notice

Once the structure becomes visible, certain moments begin to stand out differently. They no longer read as isolated frustrations, communication misses, or the normal cost of complexity. Instead, they begin to reveal where the structure is no longer carrying work cleanly and where drift has started shaping how the organization moves. You may begin to notice:

- **The capable new leader who struggles to gain traction:** A person with the skills and experience to succeed arrives and finds that progress is slower than expected. At first, this may appear to be an onboarding issue or a problem of fit. Over time, it becomes clear that the difficulty comes from accumulated ambiguity that has never been resolved. Structural gaps that others learned to navigate through workarounds become immediately visible to someone encountering them for the first time.

- **The handoff where context disappears:** Work moves from one team to another, and something essential gets lost along the way. What once looked like a communication issue begins to reveal something different. The loss is rarely random. It often marks a structural boundary where ownership was never designed to transfer cleanly and where context thins the moment work crosses over.

- **The decision that keeps getting reopened:** A choice gets made, everyone leaves aligned, and weeks later, the same issue is back on the table. What appears to be indecision is often something else. Intent did not survive the path from agreement to execution. Somewhere along the way, authority weakened, ownership blurred, or the structure failed to carry the decision forward with enough clarity to hold.

- **The initiative that weakens as it moves upward:** A decision leaves a room with clarity and returns later diluted, delayed, or reframed. What changed was not always the decision itself but the structure it had to travel through. Approval paths, governance layers, and inherited thresholds begin reshaping intent as work moves through them.

- **The escalation that should never have reached you:** A problem arrives at your level that people closer to the work should have been able to resolve. What once may have looked like hesitation or poor judgment begins to reveal something structural underneath it. Authority may be missing, ownership may be unclear, or accountability may never have been placed where the work actually lives. The place where momentum depends on presence. Decisions move once a specific person steps in. Alignment returns once someone reconnects the pieces. Momentum resumes, but only by borrowing from individual attention what the structure should have been carrying on its own.

- **The person everyone trusts because the structure cannot be trusted:** Every organization has people others rely on because they know how to move work through the system. They remember what was decided, know who to call, and can close gaps others cannot. At first, this looks like experience or leadership. Often, it is also evidence that trust has concentrated in individuals because the structure itself is no longer carrying it consistently.

None of these moments, by themselves, explain the entire organization, but they do show you where to look. They reveal where work is thinning, where structure is no longer holding, and where the visible problem may be only the surface expression of something deeper underneath.

Questions to Ask When Something Feels Heavy

Once a pattern begins to stand out, the next step is not immediate repair. The next step is learning to read the weight more accurately. These questions are not a checklist, and they are not a full diagnosis. They are simply a way of slowing down long enough to see what the structure may no longer be carrying on its own.

When something feels heavier than it should, ask:

Does authority hold under pressure, or does it collapse into escalation when a decision becomes difficult?

- Does intent survive as decisions move through the organization, or does it weaken along the way? When work crosses boundaries, does ownership transfer clearly, or does someone have to chase it to make sure it lands?

- Does momentum continue when key people are not present, or does movement depend on their involvement to hold things together?

- Does trust live in the structure itself, or has it concentrated in specific individuals who compensate for gaps others have learned to work around?

And finally:

- Who is carrying the load that the structure should have been carrying for them?

These questions do not tell you everything, but they change what you look for. They help separate the strain that belongs to growth from the strain that comes from misalignment. They do not solve the problem. They help you stop misreading it.

What This Lens Changes

The purpose of this book is not to hand you a repair sequence. It is to change how you read what is already happening inside the organization.

Once patterns of drift become visible, familiar problems stop looking isolated. Delay, escalation, rework, and fatigue no longer appear as separate failures to be fixed one at a time. They begin to read as signals coming from the same structural condition underneath.

That shift does not solve the problem on its own, but it changes the starting point. You can respond with greater accuracy. You can tell the difference between pressure that belongs to growth and weight that comes from misalignment. You can see where leadership presence is adding value and where it is compensating for structure that never learned to carry the work on its own.

That is where realignment begins. It does not start with urgency or more force, but with a clearer reading of what the organization is already telling you.

Once you can see the structure clearly, you can no longer mistake compensation for leadership or weight for execution.

For leadership teams ready to apply the Risk Stack™ inside their own organization, Layer7Risk works directly with companies to use this lens for structural diagnosis and realignment.

Please contact us at:

mindshare@layer7risk.com | layer7risk.com

About the Author

John Czapko is the creator of the Risk Stack™ and the founder of Layer7Risk, where he advises leaders on structural risk inside modern organizations. Before founding his own firms, John spent more than two decades in the enterprise technology sector, holding individual contributor and leadership roles at companies including Microsoft, Oracle, Dell, Hewlett Packard Enterprise, Symantec, Lockheed Martin, and KPMG. His work focused on complex technology environments where systems, teams, and decisions intersect across large organizations. After leaving the corporate world, John shifted his focus to risk management and founded companies dedicated to helping businesses better understand and manage their exposure. Working closely with high-growth and mid-market firms, he began noticing a recurring pattern: friction inside organizations rarely came from the problems leaders believed they were solving. Instead, the underlying structure of how work, decisions, and accountability moved through the organization had quietly drifted. Those observations eventually led to the development of the Risk Stack™, a structural lens for diagnosing where authority, ownership, accountability, and trust have fallen out of alignment. Today John works with leaders to identify structural drift so their organizations can operate with greater clarity, alignment, and momentum. John lives outside Houston, Texas with Diana and their two dogs, Willow and Emmylou. His work is grounded in a calling to bring clarity to leaders and organizations so that their work, their people, and their families can thrive.

www.ingramcontent.com/pod-product-compliance
Lightning Source LLC
Chambersburg PA
CBHW071430130726
47997CB00006B/2029